SCIENCE
Lessons & Investigations

Grade 3

Manufacturer	Evan-Moor Corporation 10 Harris Court, Suite C-3 Monterey, CA 93940, USA www.evan-moor.com
EU Rep.	Authorised Rep Compliance Ltd., Ground Floor, 71 Lower Baggot Street, Dublin, D02 P593, Ireland www.arccompliance.com

Writing: Nancy Balter
Rachel D'Orsaneo
Stacia Fletcher
Tiffany Rivera
Content Editing: Kathleen Jorgensen
Copy Editing: Cathy Harber
Art Direction: Yuki Meyer
Cover Design: Yuki Meyer
Illustration: Bryan Langdo
Design/Production: Paula Acojido
Yuki Meyer

EMC 4313

Visit
teaching-standards.com
to view a correlation
of this book.

Correlated to Current Standards

Congratulations on your purchase of some of the finest teaching materials in the world.

Photocopying the pages in this book is permitted for single-classroom use only. Making photocopies for additional classes or schools is prohibited.

For information about other Evan-Moor products, call 1-800-777-4362, fax 1-800-777-4332, or visit our website, www.evan-moor.com.

10 Harris Court, Suite C-3, Monterey, CA 93940-5773. Printed in USA.

003

CPSIA: Globus Printing & Packaging, Minster, OH, USA [2/2026]

CONTENTS

What's in *Science Lessons and Investigations*

12 Engaging Units

Science Lessons and Investigations offers 12 units on Next Generation Science Standards grade-level topics in life, earth, and physical science. Each unit follows a 5E model and includes an engagement activity, informational text and graphics, a vocabulary review, comprehension questions, and extension writing prompts and projects.

Teacher Pages

The unit begins with an overview page that provides the concept, objectives, and contents of the unit.

Next is a teacher resource page, labeled **Engage**, for you to use to introduce the concept to the class. Use it with the students' unit concept page (the student **Engage** page) to lead a discussion to elicit prior knowledge and any preconceptions. The discussion connects prior knowledge to what students will learn in the unit.

The teacher resource page also includes a "spark question" designed to capture some aspect of the topic that students may wonder about and to whet their appetite for the topic.

Lastly, the unit may include a summary of any preparation required for the Explore activity, along with any special instructions for leading the activity.

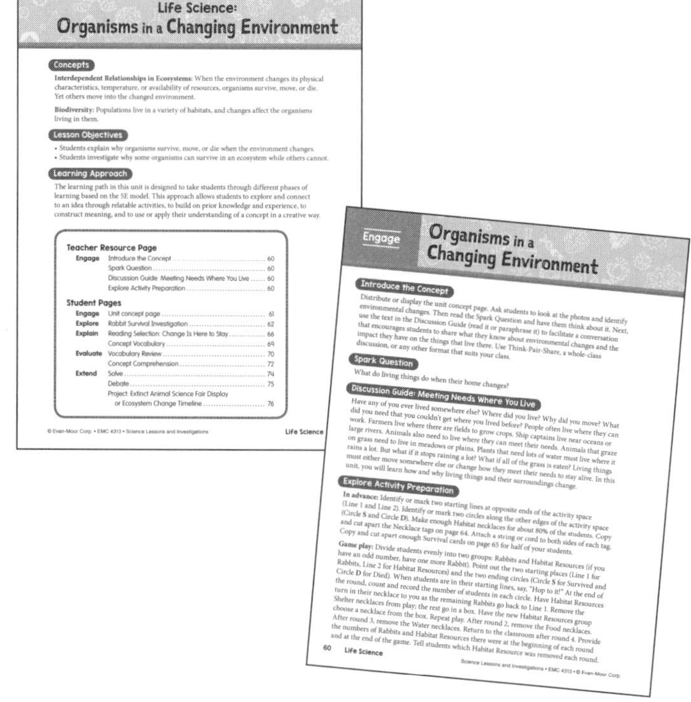

Life Science:
Organisms in a Changing Environment

Concepts

Interdependent Relationships in Ecosystems: When the environment changes its physical characteristics, temperature, or availability of resources, organisms survive, move, or die. Yet others move into the changed environment.

Biodiversity: Populations live in a variety of habitats, and changes affect the organisms living in them.

Lesson Objectives

- Students explain why organisms survive, move, or die when the environment changes.
- Students investigate why some organisms can survive in an ecosystem while others cannot.

Learning Approach

The learning path in this unit is designed to take students through different phases of learning based on the 5E model. This approach allows students to explore and connect to an idea through relatable activities, to build on prior knowledge and experience, to construct meaning, and to use or apply their understanding of a concept in a creative way.

© Evan-Moor Corp. • EMC 4313 • Science Lessons and Investigations   Life Science

Engage

Organisms in a Changing Environment

Introduce the Concept

Distribute or display the unit concept page. Ask students to look at the photos and identify environmental changes. Then read the Spark Question and have them think about it. Next, use the text in the Discussion Guide (read it or paraphrase it) to facilitate a conversation that encourages students to share what they know about environmental changes and the impact they have on the things that live there. Use Think-Pair-Share, a whole-class discussion, or any other format that suits your class.

Spark Question

What do living things do when their home changes?

Discussion Guide: Meeting Needs Where You Live

Have any of you ever lived somewhere else? Where did you live? Why did you move? What did you need that you couldn't get where you lived before? People often live where they can work. Farmers live where there are fields to grow crops. Ship captains live near oceans or large rivers. Animals also need to live where they can meet their needs. Animals that graze on grass need to live in meadows or plains. Plants that need lots of water must live where it rains a lot. But what if it stops raining a lot? What if all of the grass is eaten? Living things must either move somewhere else or change how they meet their needs to stay alive. In this unit, you will learn how and why living things and their surroundings change.

Explore Activity Preparation

In advance: Identify or mark two starting lines at opposite ends of the activity space (Line 1 and Line 2). Identify or mark two circles along the other edges of the activity space (Circle **S** and Circle **D**). Make enough Habitat necklaces for about 80% of the students. Copy and cut apart the Necklace tags on page 64. Attach a string or cord to both sides of each tag. Copy and cut apart enough Survival cards on page 65 for half of your students.

Game play: Divide students evenly into two groups: Rabbits and Habitat Resources (if you have an odd number, have one more Rabbit). Point out the two starting places (Line 1 for Rabbits, Line 2 for Habitat Resources) and the two ending circles (Circle **S** for Survived and Circle **D** for Died). When students are in their starting lines, say, "Hop to it!" At the end of the round, count and record the number of students in each circle. Have Habitat Resources turn in their necklace to you as the remaining Rabbits go back to Line 1. Remove the Shelter necklaces from play; the rest go in a box. Have the new Habitat Resources group choose a necklace from the box. Repeat play. After round 2, remove the Food necklaces. After round 3, remove the Water necklaces. Return to the classroom after round 4. Provide the numbers of Rabbits and Habitat Resources there were at the beginning of each round and at the end of the game. Tell students which Habitat Resource was removed each round.

60 Life Science   Science Lessons and Investigations • EMC 4313 • © Evan-Moor Corp.

Unit Concept Page

This page is used during the concept introduction to provide relevant visuals and examples that will be used in the discussion. The page may also be used in some of the Explore activities.

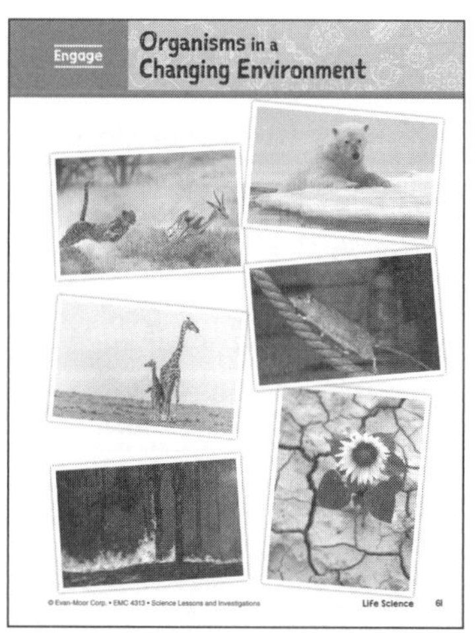

Explore Activity

These student pages help students make a hands-on connection to one aspect of the concept. Students usually work in small groups to explore, investigate, model, or experiment and record their data and observations. They are often prompted to come up with a preliminary explanation, which they can refine as the unit progresses. Please provide students with the materials listed before they begin the activity.

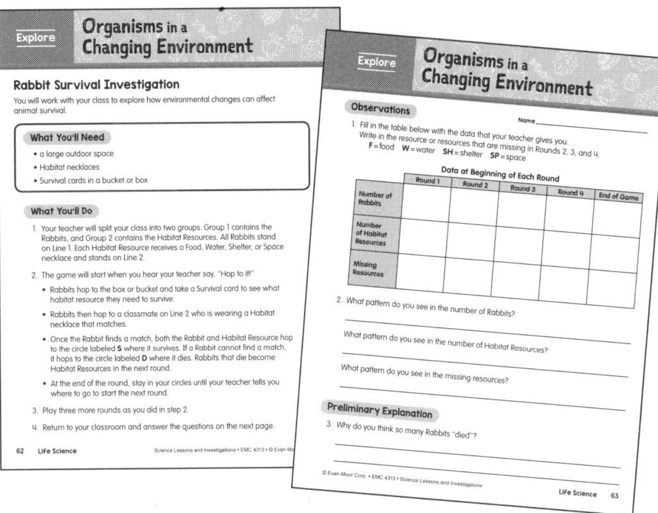

Explore — Organisms in a Changing Environment

Rabbit Survival Investigation

You will work with your class to explore how environmental changes can affect animal survival.

What You'll Need

- a large outdoor space
- Habitat necklaces
- Survival cards in a bucket or box

What You'll Do

1. Your teacher will split your class into two groups. Group 1 contains the Rabbits, and Group 2 contains the Habitat Resources. All Rabbits stand on Line 1. Each Habitat Resource receives a Food, Water, Shelter, or Space necklace and stands on Line 2.
2. The game will start when you hear your teacher say, "Hop to it!"
   - Rabbits hop to the box or bucket and take a Survival card to see what habitat resource they need to survive.
   - Rabbits then hop to a classmate on Line 2 who is wearing a Habitat necklace that matches.
   - Once the Rabbit finds a match, both the Rabbit and Habitat Resource hop to the circle labeled **S** where it survives. If a Rabbit cannot find a match, it hops to the circle labeled **D** where it dies. Rabbits that die become Habitat Resources in the next round.
   - At the end of the round, stay in your circles until your teacher tells you where to go to start the next round.
3. Play three more rounds as you did in step 2.
4. Return to your classroom and answer the questions on the next page.

62 Life Science — Science Lessons and Investigations • EMC 4313 • © Evan-Mo[or Corp.]

Explore — Organisms in a Changing Environment

Observations Name ______

1. Fill in the table below with the data that your teacher gives you. Write in the resource or resources that are missing in Rounds 2, 3, and 4:
   F = food **W** = water **SH** = shelter **SP** = space

Data at Beginning of Each Round

	Round 1	Round 2	Round 3	Round 4	End of Game
Number of Rabbits					
Number of Habitat Resources					
Missing Resources					

2. What pattern do you see in the number of Rabbits?
   What pattern do you see in the number of Habitat Resources?
   What pattern do you see in the missing resources?

Preliminary Explanation

3. Why do you think so many Rabbits "died"?

© Evan-Moor Corp. • EMC 4313 • Science Lessons and Investigations — Life Science 63

Reading Selection

These pages provide students with information about the concept along with photos, illustrations, diagrams, graphs, or other visual support.

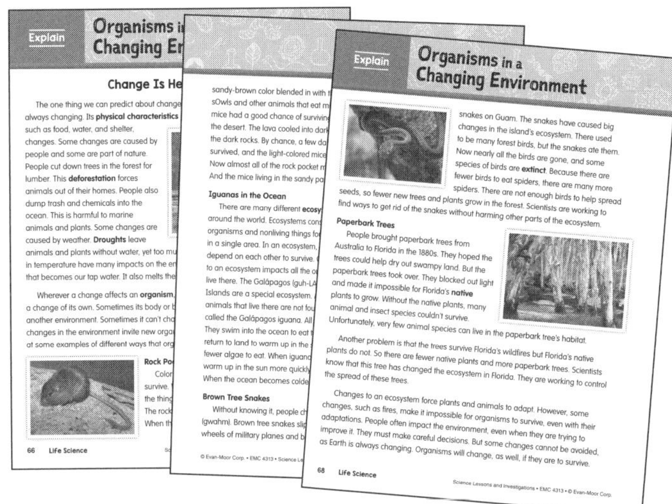

Explain — Organisms in a Changing Environment

snakes on Guam. The snakes have caused big changes in the island's ecosystem. There used to be many forest birds, but the snakes ate them. Now nearly all the birds are gone, and some species of birds are **extinct**. Because there are fewer birds to eat spiders, there are many more spiders. There are not enough birds to help spread seeds, so fewer new trees and plants grow in the forest. Scientists are working to find ways to get rid of the snakes without harming other parts of the ecosystem.

Paperbark Trees

People brought paperbark trees from Australia to Florida in the 1880s. They hoped the trees could help dry out swampy land. But the paperbark trees took over. They blocked out light and made it impossible for Florida's **native** plants to grow. Without the native plants, many animal and insect species couldn't survive. Unfortunately, very few animal species can live in the paperbark tree's habitat.

Another problem is that the trees survive Florida's wildfires but Florida's native plants do not. So there are fewer native plants and more paperbark trees. Scientists know that this tree has changed the ecosystem in Florida. They are working to control the spread of these trees.

Changes to an ecosystem force plants and animals to adapt. However, some changes, such as fires, make it impossible for organisms to survive, even with their adaptations. People often impact the environment, even when they are trying to improve it. They must make careful decisions. But some changes cannot be avoided, as Earth is always changing. Organisms will change, as well, if they are to survive.

68 Life Science — Science Lessons and Investigations • EMC 4313 • © Evan-Moor Corp.

Concept Vocabulary and Vocabulary Review

Highlighted terms presented in context in the reading selection are defined. The Concept Vocabulary page can be used as a resource throughout the unit. There is a section of the page that can be used as a practice activity of your choosing, such as using the terms in sentences or listing examples of each term. The Vocabulary Review page(s) allow students to connect with the meaning of the term beyond just matching it with its definition.

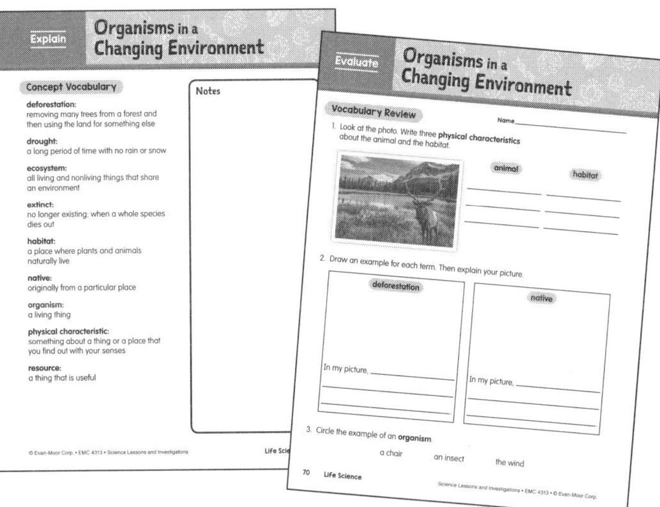

Explain — Organisms in a Changing Environment

Concept Vocabulary

deforestation: removing many trees from a forest and then using the land for something else

drought: a long period of time with no rain or snow

ecosystem: all living and nonliving things that share an environment

extinct: no longer existing; when a whole species dies out

habitat: a place where plants and animals naturally live

native: originally from a particular place

organism: a living thing

physical characteristic: something about a thing or a place that you find out with your senses

resource: a thing that is useful

Notes

© Evan-Moor Corp. • EMC 4313 • Science Lessons and Investigations — Life Sci[ence]

Evaluate — Organisms in a Changing Environment

Vocabulary Review Name ______

1. Look at the photo. Write three **physical characteristics** about the animal and the habitat.
   animal | habitat
2. Draw an example for each term. Then explain your picture.
   deforestation — In my picture, ______
   native — In my picture, ______
3. Circle the example of an **organism**.
   a chair an insect the wind

70 Life Science — Science Lessons and Investigations • EMC 4313 • © Evan-Moor Corp.

Concept Comprehension

Students answer questions about what they have learned so far. Students write out their answers for most questions, and many require higher-order thinking.

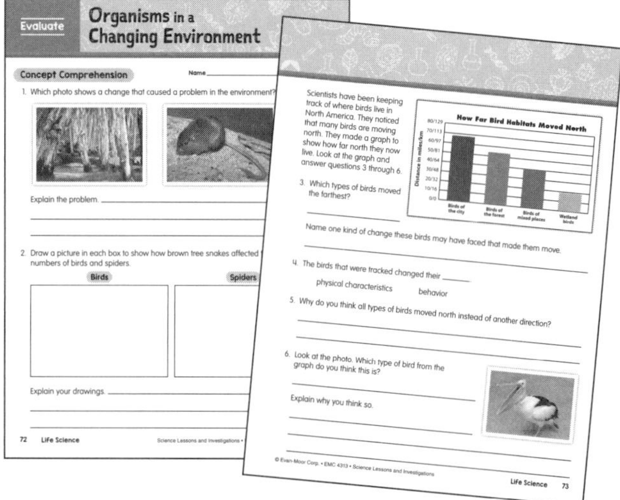
Evaluate
Organisms in a Changing Environment

Concept Comprehension Name

1. Which photo shows a change that caused a problem in the environment?

Explain the problem.

2. Draw a picture in each box to show how brown tree snakes affected numbers of birds and spiders.

Birds Spiders

Explain your drawings.

72 Life Science Science Lessons and Investigations •

Scientists have been keeping track of where birds live in North America. They noticed that many birds are moving north. They made a graph to show how far north they now live. Look at the graph and answer questions 3 through 6.

3. Which types of birds moved the farthest?

Name one kind of change these birds may have faced that made them move.

4. The birds that were tracked changed their
physical characteristics behavior

5. Why do you think all types of birds moved north instead of another direction?

6. Look at the photo. Which type of bird from the graph do you think this is?

Explain why you think so.

© Evan-Moor Corp. • EMC 4313 • Science Lessons and Investigations Life Science 73

Extend Writing Prompts

Students apply, reflect, analyze, invent, or otherwise use what they've learned to complete a task. Their response may involve writing, drawing, and/or diagramming.

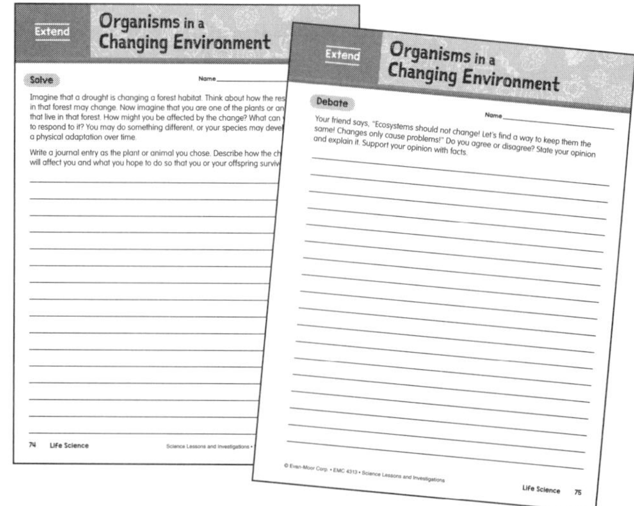
Extend
Organisms in a Changing Environment

Solve Name

Imagine that a drought is changing a forest habitat. Think about how the res[t] in that forest may change. Now imagine that you are one of the plants or an[imals] that live in that forest. How might you be affected by the change? What can [you do] to respond to it? You may do something different, or your species may devel[op] a physical adaptation over time.

Write a journal entry as the plant or animal you chose. Describe how the ch[ange] will affect you and what you hope to do so that you or your offspring surviv[e].

74 Life Science Science Lessons and Investigations •

Extend
Organisms in a Changing Environment

Debate Name

Your friend says, "Ecosystems should not change! Let's find a way to keep them the same! Changes only cause problems!" Do you agree or disagree? State your opinion and explain it. Support your opinion with facts.

© Evan-Moor Corp. • EMC 4313 • Science Lessons and Investigations Life Science 75

Projects

Two different types of open-ended, hands-on projects are offered for students to choose from. They may allow students to further investigate some aspect of the concept, integrate with another content area, create or invent something, or design an experiment. Students have control over the projects they produce, many of which are real-world products. Some projects lend themselves to working in groups, and most can be done individually.

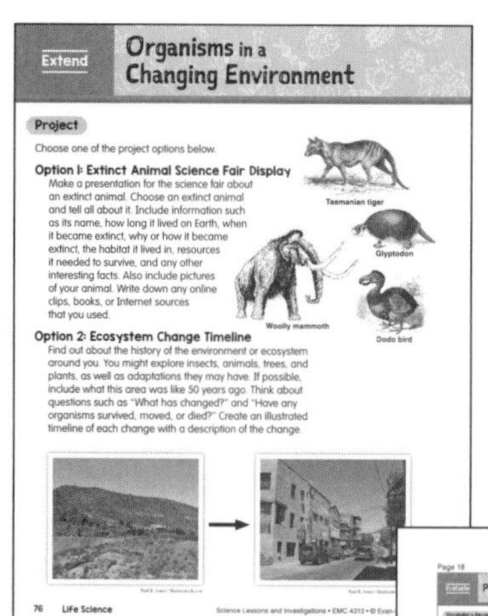
Extend
Organisms in a Changing Environment

Project

Choose one of the project options below.

Option 1: Extinct Animal Science Fair Display
Make a presentation for the science fair about an extinct animal. Choose an extinct animal and tell all about it. Include information such as its name, how long it lived on Earth, when it became extinct, why or how it became extinct, the habitat it lived in, resources it needed to survive, and any other interesting facts. Also include pictures of your animal. Write down any online clips, books, or Internet sources that you used.

Option 2: Ecosystem Change Timeline
Find out about the history of the environment or ecosystem around you. You might explore insects, animals, trees, and plants, as well as adaptations they may have. If possible, include what this area was like 50 years ago. Think about questions such as "What has changed?" and "Have any organisms survived, moved, or died?" Create an illustrated timeline of each change with a description of the change.

76 Life Science Science Lessons and Investigations • EMC 4313 • © Evan-Moor

Answer Key

Answers are provided for the Vocabulary Review and Concept Comprehension pages. The correct answer or an exemplar response is shown, unless the question is completely open-ended. All other student pages are open-ended. You may establish your own criteria for evaluating work.

How to Use *Science Lessons and Investigations* in Your Classroom

Teaching Strategies

- Identify a topic or concept for your class to work on. Read through the unit and decide which parts, if not all, that your students need.
- Reproduce the pages in the unit that students will use. Include the Concept Vocabulary page, which defines key concept terms. Have students keep it in their science notebooks or portfolios or tape it to their desks for easy reference.
- Group students as specified for the Explore activity. For other activities, have students work independently, with a partner, or in small groups.
- If you send a page home for homework, send the Concept Vocabulary page for support, as well.
- Allow sufficient time for sharing and discussing results, observations, ideas, answers, and projects. Real-world science involves cooperation and learning from each other.

Keep in Mind

Science involves creative thinking, attention to detail, and observation based on the senses, not preconceived notions or what students think is expected. For hands-on activities, accept all data and observations as valid even if they indicate a likely procedural problem, mishap, or other issue. Have students compare results, and challenge students to come up with a reason for significant discrepancies.

Science involves asking questions about how the world works and trying to find the answers. While we already know some of these answers and provide them to young people, we do not want to give the impression that science is just learning facts. Much of real-world science actually involves constructive failure, in which potential answers are tested and found to be incorrect. Non-answers are a valuable part of the trek toward understanding. Downplay errors while reinforcing correct procedures and habits and attempts at reasoning.

Science Materials Needed

Dear Parent/Guardian,

Our class is doing a science activity on ______________________________.
(date)

Can you please provide the following materials by the date above?

____________________________ ____________________________

____________________________ ____________________________

Thank you!

Sincerely,

____________________________, Room __________

Tips for Science Activities

Follow the procedures as best you can and record what happens. When you explore, investigate, or experiment, there are no right or wrong answers.

Science is about trial and error. If something doesn't work, you've learned a little more about it. Try something different next time.

Creativity is sometimes needed to come up with new ideas to test or ways to investigate something.

The Nature of Science

- Science tries to answer questions about the natural world. It is a way of knowing.
- Investigations use many methods.
- Knowledge is based on evidence and is updated when new evidence is found.
- Science assumes there is a reason for each natural event, even if we don't yet know what it is.
- Models, laws, and theories explain natural events.

Life Science:

Plant and Animal Life Cycles

Concept

Growth and Development of Organisms: Reproduction is essential to the continued existence of every kind of organism. Plants and animals have unique and diverse life cycles.

Lesson Objectives

- Students will conclude why reproduction is an integral component of plant and animal survival.
- Students will explain the similarities and differences between plant and animal life cycles.

Learning Approach

The learning path in this unit is designed to take students through different phases of learning based on the 5E model. This approach allows students to explore and connect to an idea through relatable activities, to build on prior knowledge and experience, to construct meaning, and to use or apply their understanding of a concept in a creative way.

Teacher Resource Page

Student Pages

Engage

Plant and Animal Life Cycles

Introduce the Concept

Distribute or display the unit concept page. Ask students to look at the pictures and think about plant and animal life cycles. Notice the changes that each plant or animal goes through. Then read the Spark Question to students and ask them to think about it. Next, use the text in the Discussion Guide (read it or paraphrase it) to facilitate a conversation that encourages students to share what they know about what happens during plant and animal life cycles. Use Think-Pair-Share, a whole-class discussion, or any other format that suits your class.

Spark Question

How does a plant or an animal grow differently from how you grow?

Discussion Guide: Different Life Cycles for Different Lives

Plants, animals, and humans all grow differently. However, all living things follow a specific life cycle. Do you know what a life cycle is? Animals and plants are born or sprout, grow, reproduce, and then they die. Do any parts of these cycles happen at the same time? Certain animals completely change shape during their life. Can you find any examples on the Engage page? Which life cycle do you think is closest to a human life cycle? Do other things happen during a cycle? In this unit, you will learn about different life cycles. You will see the changes that some plants and animals go through at each different stage.

Explore Activity Preparation

Plan an area with ample sunlight for students to put their plants for two weeks. At the end of the activity, determine what will be done with all of the plants. You might let students plant them in an outside garden at school, continue observing them in the classroom, or take them home.

Engage

Plant and Animal Life Cycles

tomato plant life cycle

duck life cycle

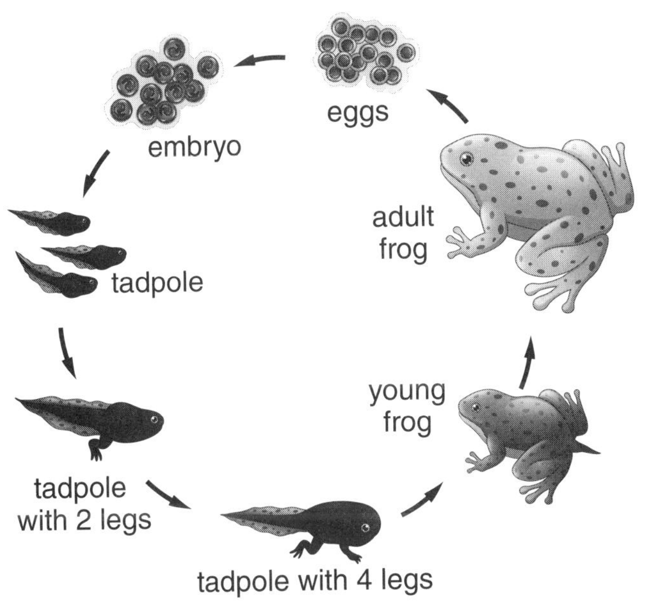

frog life cycle

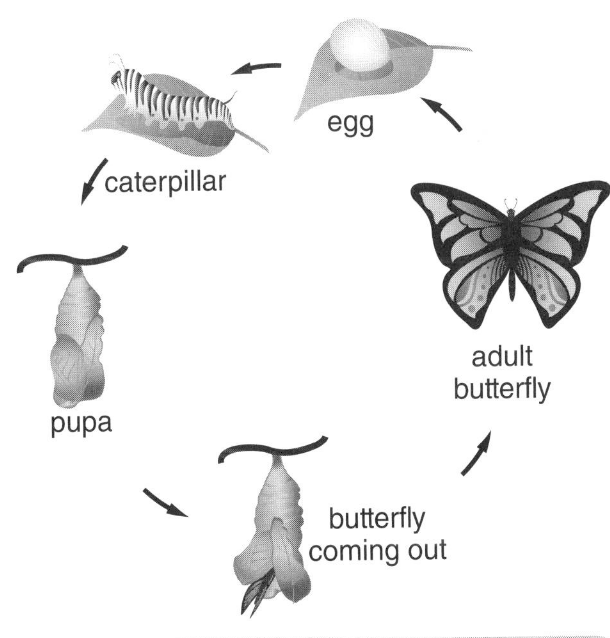

butterfly life cycle

Plant Life Cycle Observation

You will work in pairs to explore the different stages of two different plants' life cycles and growth.

What You'll Need

- three small clear cups
- a permanent marker
- soil
- a radish seed
- a marigold seed
- water
- a pencil

What You'll Do

1. Use a permanent marker to label one cup **Marigold** and the other cup **Radish**. Write today's date and your names on the cup, as well.
2. Put soil in both cups. Then plant each seed in its cup. Push the seed about a half inch (1 centimeter) down into the soil. Use the third cup to give both of your plants a small amount of water and place them near a window where they can get sunlight.
3. Make a prediction about when each plant will sprout and how big each will get. Write your predictions at the top of the next page.
4. Water your plants a little every day for two weeks.
5. Twice a week, observe your plants. Draw a picture of each plant on the next page. Then write a sentence about what you see.
6. After your last observation, answer the questions on page 14.

Explore

Plant and Animal Life Cycles

Predictions

Name ____________________

I predict the marigold will sprout ____________________.

I predict the radish will sprout ____________________.

Observations

Date	Marigold drawing	Radish drawing	Observations

Plant and Animal Life Cycles

Analysis

1. Were your predictions correct? Explain.

2. What did the marigold look like at the end of Week 2?

   What did the radish plant look like at the end of Week 2?

3. What did your plants need to have in order to grow?

4. What similarities and differences do you notice between the marigold and radish plants?

5. How do your plants look different from these adult plants?

radish

marigold

Explain

Plant and Animal Life Cycles

A Seed, An Egg, or Mom

Plant Life Cycles

A seed doesn't look like the plant it will become. But inside are the tiny beginnings of a root and a stem. The seed has a food supply, too. A seed coat covers and protects everything inside the seed.

When the **conditions** are right, the seeds will **germinate**. At this **stage** of the plant's life, roots and a stem poke out from inside the seed. Warmth from the sun, water from the rain, and food from the soil are the right conditions for the seedling's growth.

As a plant grows taller, it also grows new parts. Its new leaves help make food for the plant. New roots hold it in the soil. Many plants develop flowers.

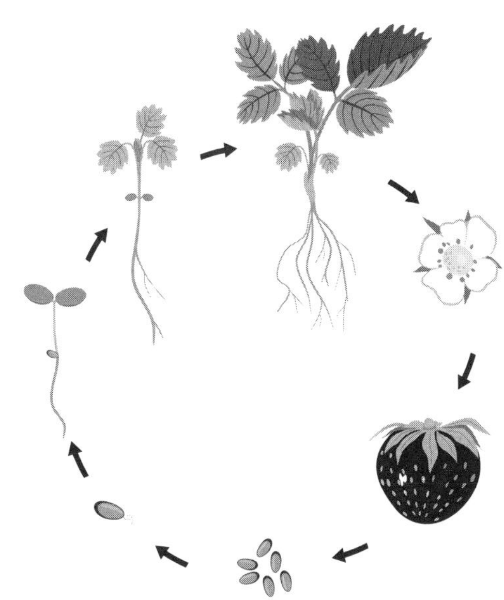

Some flowers make fruit to put their seeds in.

Flowers are beautiful to look at and they smell good. But they also do important work for the plant. Flowers make seeds, which are needed for the plant to **reproduce**, or make new plants. Sometimes the seeds drop to the ground. Other seeds are carried away and dropped by animals or by the wind. Many flowering plants produce their seeds and then die. When the conditions are right, the seeds will produce new plants. A whole new **life cycle** will begin.

Flowers make seeds when pollen travels from one flower to the seed-making part of another. Insects such as bees, moths, and butterflies help carry pollen from flower to flower. When an insect lands on a flower, pollen sticks to it. When the insect visits another flower, some of the pollen falls off its body and **pollinates** that flower.

Plant and Animal Life Cycles

Animal Life Cycles

Some animals have babies just like people do. Many animal babies, like dogs and horses, grow in their mother's body. Other animal mothers, like chickens and frogs, lay eggs on the ground or in water. A baby grows inside each egg. As babies, some animals look just like their parents. Others look very different as they grow because they go through **metamorphosis**, a kind of change. For example, a caterpillar changes into a butterfly.

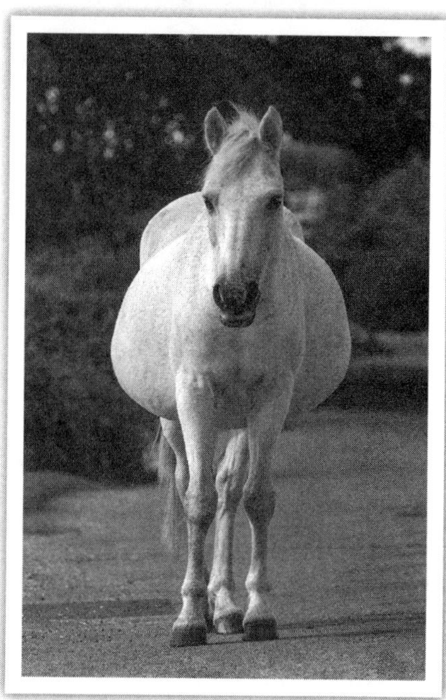

A baby horse grows inside this mother horse.

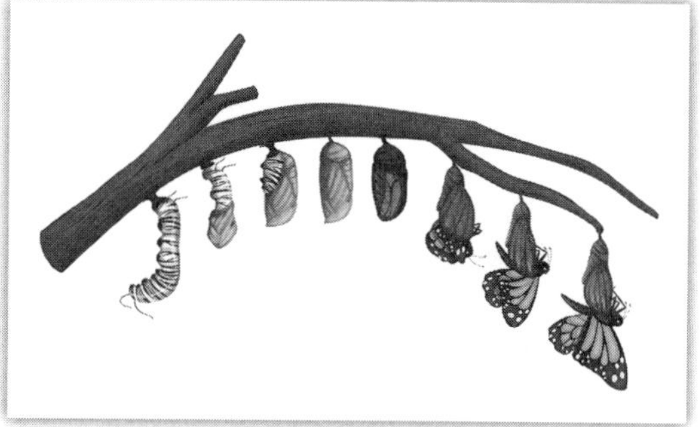

A caterpillar's metamorphosis into a butterfly

Once the babies are born or hatch, most animals need an adult to show them how to survive. They need shelter and food. An adult animal can help them find safety, along with food and water for **sustenance**. As they grow and get older, they need less guidance from an adult. When they become adults, they can reproduce and have babies. The entire process starts all over.

A baby orangutan travels on its mother's back. She is teaching it how to find food and build a nest.

Plants and animals have similarities and differences in their life cycles. Both are born or begin to sprout. Then they grow and reproduce. But while plants start from a seed, animals start inside their mothers' bodies or from an egg that the mother lays. At the end of the life cycle, both plants and animals die. But the process starts all over again, because they've left a piece of themselves behind to continue living!

Explain

Plant and Animal Life Cycles

Concept Vocabulary

conditions: things that affect how something happens

germinate: to begin to grow; to sprout

life cycle: the stages that a living thing goes through during its life

metamorphosis: a big change in an animal's form between its early life and becoming an adult

pollinate: to bring pollen to a plant

reproduce: to produce babies, or offspring

stage: a step in a process

sustenance: what is needed for survival

Notes

Plant and Animal Life Cycles

Vocabulary Review

Name ______________________________

1. Look at the diagram and the terms in the word box below. Circle the terms that the diagram represents.

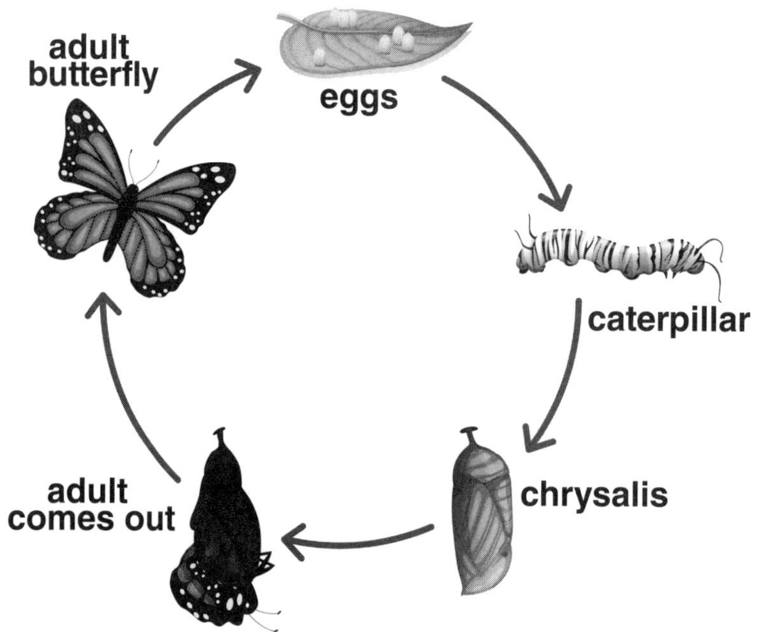

sustenance	germinate	life cycle
metamorphosis	conditions	stage

Explain each word you chose.

____

____

____

____

2. Circle the concept vocabulary term that correctly completes the sentence.

When Rita's dog _______, she had six puppies!

germinated **reproduced** **pollinated**

3. Look at the pair of photos in each box. Write the concept vocabulary term they illustrate.

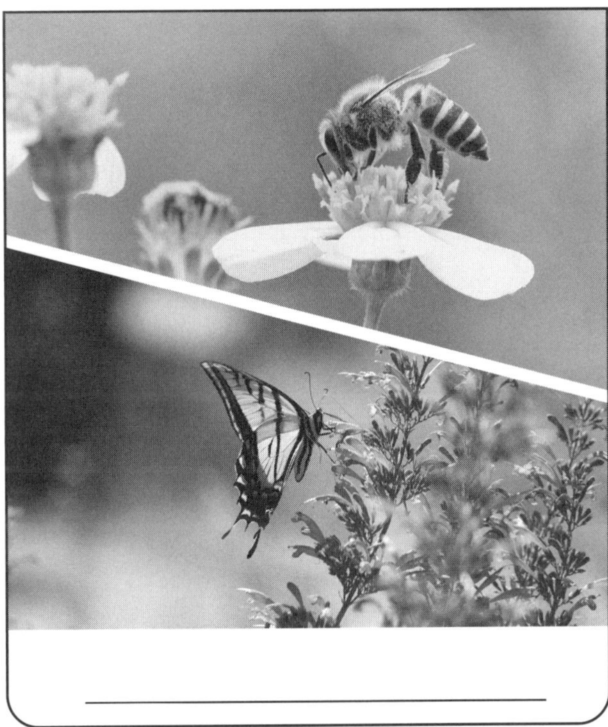

Evaluate

Plant and Animal Life Cycles

Concept Comprehension

Name ________________________________

1. What are two similarities of plant and animal life cycles?

____

____

____

2. What are two differences between plant and animal life cycles?

____

____

____

3. Read the title of the diagram. Draw a picture in each box to complete it.

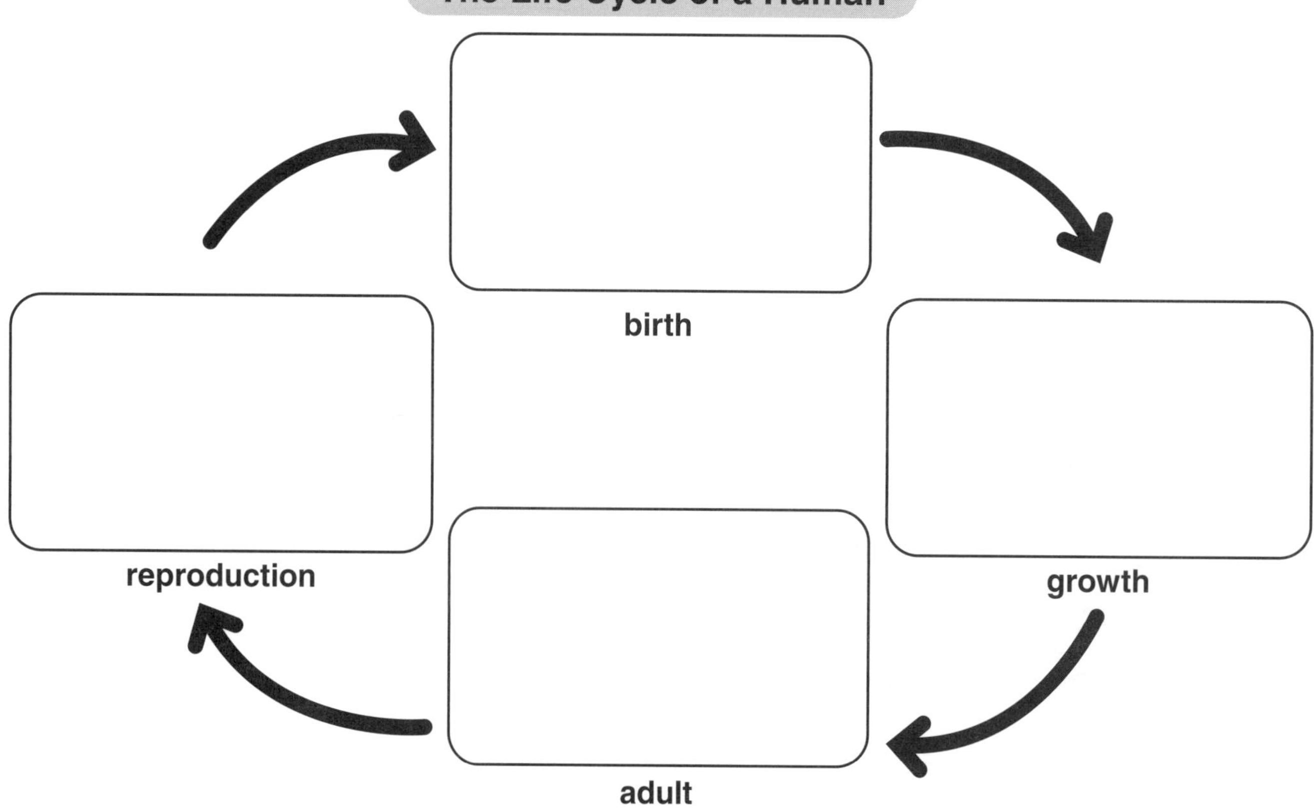

Evaluate

Plant and Animal Life Cycles

4. Is metamorphosis involved in all life cycles? Explain your answer and include examples.

____

____

____

____

5. Read the incorrect sentence. Write the sentence correctly on the line.

   Flowers make roots and use them to reproduce.

____

6. Complete the Venn diagram to compare an egg and a seed.

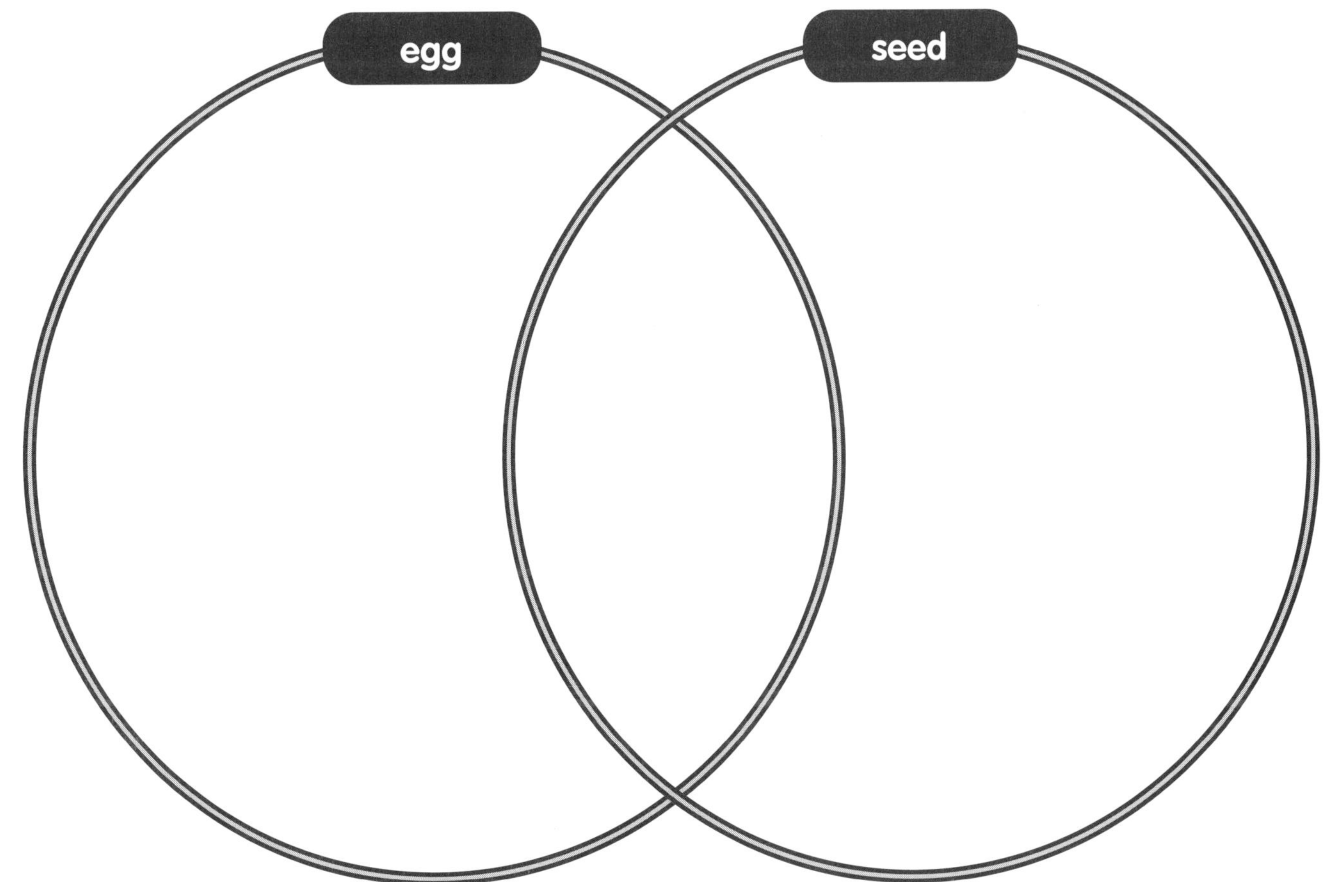

Extend

Plant and Animal Life Cycles

Imagine

Name ______________________________

Look at the turtle life cycle and imagine that you are a turtle. Choose a stage to start at and imagine that you are about to enter the next stage. Write a journal entry that describes what you are experiencing. Think about what it would be like in both stages, how it would feel, and what different things you would do in both stages.

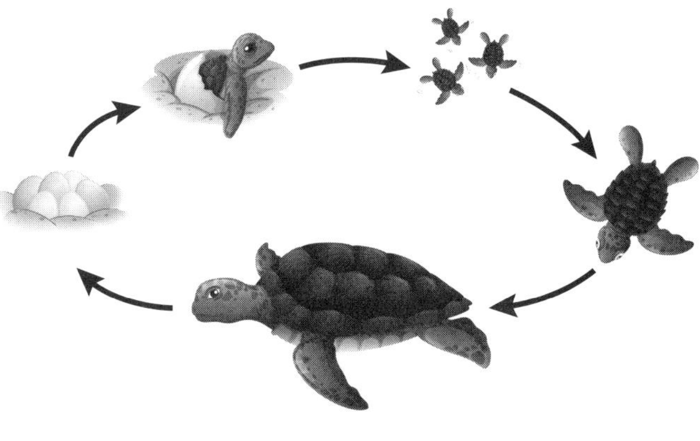

____

____

____

____

____

____

____

____

____

____

____

____

____

____

____

Extend

Plant and Animal Life Cycles

Explain

Name ______________________________

Your teacher has some bad news. He announces, "There are no longer any roses in the entire world! They are all gone!" If there were no more roses anywhere in the world, explain what could have happened to cause this.

Extend

Plant and Animal Life Cycles

Project

Choose one of the project options below.

Option 1: Life Cycle Video

Work with a partner or a group to create a video of the life cycle of your favorite animal. Find books and other resources to help you learn about your animal and how it grows. Write a script to present the facts about your animal. Then act out your animal's life cycle. Have someone record your group as you act and present your information, or perform it live. Use props to help you act out each stage. If needed, create the props you need.

Option 2: Seed Mosaic

A mosaic is a type of art made using small colored objects to make shapes. Draw an outline of a beautiful plant, flower, tree, or bush on a sheet of paper. You can draw one that is in your neighborhood or a park, one that you have seen in a magazine or online, or one from your imagination. Think about the different colors and shades of color in different parts of the plant. Mark where different colors will go. Then find seeds in the colors you need or buy them in a store. Notice all the different sizes and textures of the seeds, and think about how to use the differences in your mosaic. Once you've planned where the seeds are going, start gluing them onto your drawing close together so that they fill in the entire outlined space. It's a new way to "grow" a plant from seeds!

Life Science: Nature and Nurture

Concept

Inheritance of Traits: Organisms inherit many characteristics from their parents. Other characteristics result from individuals' interactions with the environment. Many characteristics involve both inheritance and the environment.

Lesson Objectives

- Students discover the roles of heredity and the environment on how organisms develop.
- Students determine which traits are most likely inherited, learned, or both.

Learning Approach

The learning path in this unit is designed to take students through different phases of learning based on the 5E model. This approach allows students to explore and connect to an idea through relatable activities, to build on prior knowledge and experience, to construct meaning, and to use or apply their understanding of a concept in a creative way.

Teacher Resource Page

Student Pages

Engage

Nature and Nurture

Introduce the Concept

Distribute or display the unit concept page and have students study the families in the photos. Read the Spark Question and ask students to think about it. Ask students how they can tell that these are families. Elicit similarities and differences between the family members in each photo. Next, use the text in the Discussion Guide (read it or paraphrase it) to facilitate a conversation that encourages students to describe themselves and their close family members, both in how they look and how they act. Use Think-Pair-Share, a whole-class discussion, or any other format that suits your class.

Spark Question

How are people like their parents but also different from them?

Discussion Guide: A Family Portrait

Think about what you have in common with either of your parents. Do you have the same color hair, eyes, or skin as one of them? Are you both extra tall or short? Is the shape of your nose, ears, or face similar? How about your smile or laugh or the way you speak? Are there talents or interests that you and either of your parents share? If you have any brothers or sisters, compare yourself to them. In what ways are you similar?

Now think about differences between you and other family members. In what ways are you unique? If you have the same hair, eye, and skin color, how can people tell you apart? Do you act differently in the same situation? Do you choose different kinds of friends than your brothers or sisters choose? Are you the best at something in your family?

Note: *Adjust questions accordingly if there are students who don't know their biological parents.*

Explore Activity Preparation

Plan how to divide your class into groups of three or four students. Photocopy the animal cards on pages 30 and 31. Each group will receive one animal card, with each group member receiving a copy of the same card. Cut out and group the cards.

The Predictions section uses the card with cats on it. Plan to project or distribute this card to all students after the Observations portion has been completed.

Nature and Nurture

Explore

Nature and Nurture

Select a Pet Observation

You will work in groups of three or four to examine differences in traits in animal families.

What You'll Need

- a set of animal cards, one card for each person in your group
- a magnifying glass
- a pencil

What You'll Do

1. You get to choose a pet from the animals on your group's card!
    - Look carefully at each animal on the card.
    - Use the magnifying glass if you need to look more closely at any details.
    - Decide which animal you would like best as a pet. Keep your choice secret from the other members of your group.
2. Complete the Observations section on the next page. Answer the first question and then write a detailed description of the animal you chose. Your description should be clear enough to tell the owner of the animals exactly which one to bring to you. Don't mention where the animal is in the photo, because the owner doesn't have the photo.
3. After everyone in your group has written his or her description, each of you will trade descriptions with another member of your group. Take turns reading the descriptions aloud. See if you can figure out which animal your groupmate chose. If you guess wrong, ask the person who wrote the description to add more detail. Then guess again.
4. Then complete the Predictions questions on the next page, using the card with cats on it.

Explore

Nature and Nurture

Observations

Name ____________________

1. What do all of the animals in the photo have in common?

2. Describe the animal you chose. Use details that tell how your animal is unique.

Predictions

3. Look at the card with cats on it. All the kittens have the same parents. What do you think the parents look like?

4. Which traits do you think were passed down from the parent cats to their kittens?

Select a Pet Animal Cards

hedgehogs

cats

rabbits

chickens

Select a Pet Animal Cards

pigs

horses

goats

Nature and Nurture

Becoming Who We Are

There are many different kinds of plants and animals, including people. They all produce **offspring**, or young versions of themselves. The offspring grow up to **resemble**, or look like, their parents. Offspring **inherit**, or receive, some of their **traits**, or features, from both of their parents. Some animals, such as bears, start life looking very much like an adult, just much smaller. A young grizzly bear has brown fur, four thick legs, and a large head with two small ears, just like its parents. Other animals, like butterflies, change a lot during their life. Butterflies start out looking like worms that hatch from an egg! But as adults, butterflies look like their parents.

Even though we inherit traits from our parents, we don't look *exactly* like either one of them. We might have a nose like our dad and freckles like our mom. But our hair may be in between Mom's straight brown hair and Dad's curly blond hair.

This mother and daughter have the same shaped eyes, nose, and chin.

Other traits that we inherit affect how our bodies **function**, or work. For example, if one of your parents wears glasses or contact lenses, you might need to wear them, as well. Allergies can also be inherited. If you sneeze when certain plants are in bloom, one of your parents probably does, too. If parent apple trees produce apples that are super crunchy, trees grown from those seeds will probably produce crunchy apples, as well.

All of these traits that we are born with come from **nature**. But there are many other traits that make us unique.

Traits that come from **nurture** are traits we get from the world around us. They are changes from things we **experience**, or that happen to us. But our offspring will not have these traits. Some of these traits play a role in how we look. An athlete develops stronger muscles by working out. A skier gets a broken bone in an accident. The children of the athlete and skier will not inherit these traits.

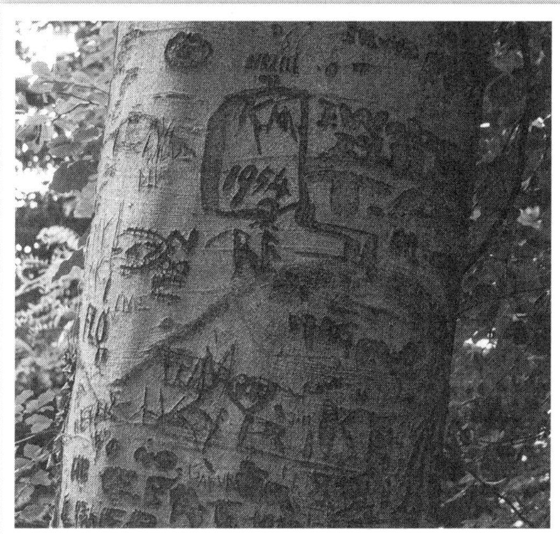

People have carved graffiti on this tree trunk. The tree will have these scars its whole life, but it will not pass them on to a baby tree.

Nurture plays an even bigger role in what we are like than in how we look. Most traits that come from nurture affect our brains. Everything we learn to do and every talent we use comes from nurture. You may be good at reading because your parents read to you every day when you were a baby. You may be a talented cook because you tried lots of foods when you were younger.

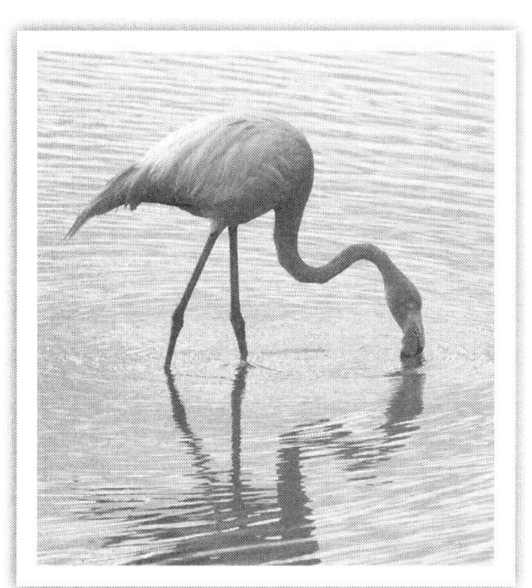

Many traits are a combination of nature and nurture. For example, flamingos are a bright orange-pink bird, but they don't inherit their color. Instead, flamingos inherit a taste for shrimp. It's their diet of orange-pink shrimp that gives flamingos their special color. Another example is height, a trait that you inherit from your parents. But what you eat as a child can also affect how you grow. Eating certain foods, such as milk, can make bones grow longer. How we function can also be a combination of nature and nurture. If you take piano or violin lessons and practice a lot, you can be very musical. If you were born with long fingers, playing these instruments could be easier. No matter what traits nature gave you at birth, there is probably a way to nurture them to be whatever you want.

Explain

Nature and Nurture

Concept Vocabulary

experience:
to do something; to have something happen to you

function:
to work; to do what it is supposed to do

inherit:
to receive something from someone else

nature:
traits a living thing is born with; basic qualities that a living thing has

nurture:
what happens to a living thing after it is born; the way a living thing is raised

offspring:
children; the young of any plant or animal

resemble:
to look or act like

trait:
a feature; a quality; a characteristic

Notes

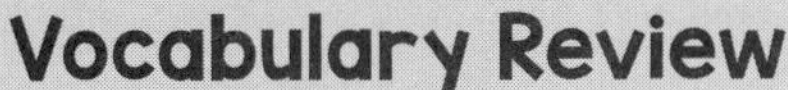

Nature and Nurture

Vocabulary Review

Name ______________________________

1. Complete the model for the term **offspring**.

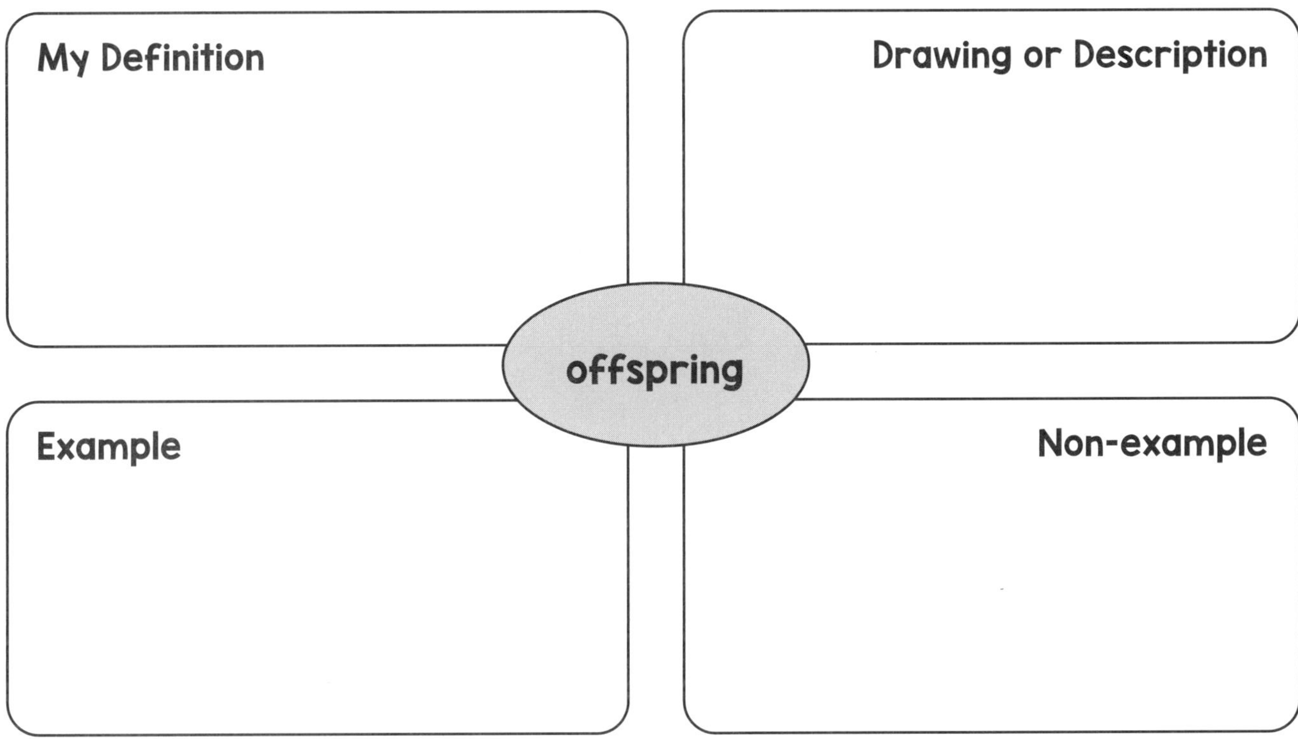

2. Some traits affect how living things look.

   Other traits affect how living things ____________________.

3. Which of these is an example of a trait? Circle it.

   a heart-shaped leaf　　a brother or sister　　playing baseball

4. Draw a line to show which words go with **nature**, **nurture**, or both.

   nature　　**nurture**

   experience　　inherit　　resemble　　trait

Nature and Nurture

Concept Comprehension

Name ______________________________

1. Circle the offspring of an orange tree.

2. Joy wrote these statements in science class:

   All the traits we inherit affect how we look.

   All the traits we get from experience affect how we function.

   Are her statements correct? ______________

   If "yes," explain why. If "no," rewrite the statements so they are correct.

   ____

   ____

   ____

3. Look at this sheep. Write two traits the sheep inherited.

   ____

   ____

   Write a trait the sheep got after it was born.

   ____

   ____

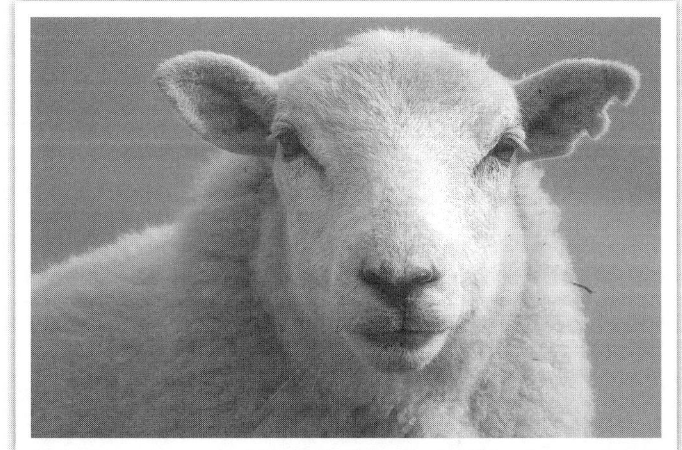

4. Look at these photos of a mother and her puppies.

Which traits do you think the puppies got from their mother?

____

____

What do you think the puppies' father might look like? Explain why.

____

____

____

____

5. Which of these is a trait of a flowering plant that is inherited? Circle your answer.

the health of the leaves   the amount of water they get   the number of petals

6. Which of these is a trait of a fruit tree that comes from experience? Circle your answer.

the type of fruit it makes   the number of leaves bugs eat   the size of its seeds

7. Which of these is a trait of a racehorse that comes from both experience and its parents? Circle your answer.

the speed it can run   the color of its mane and tail   the bruise on its leg

Nature and Nurture

Wonder

Name ______________________

Have you ever wondered what it would be like if every person looked and behaved exactly the same? How might this be helpful? How might this be confusing? What problems could it cause? How would a community's needs be met? Explain your thoughts and include examples. Use vocabulary and concepts from this unit.

Extend

Nature and Nurture

Imagine

Name ______________________

Imagine you are a 9-year-old human who is being raised by a grizzly bear in a forest. Do you think it would be helpful or harmful to look so different from your bear parent? How easy would it be to learn how to live in the forest like a bear? Write a story describing what your life would be like. Include things that you'd do every day.

Extend

Nature and Nurture

Project

Choose one of the project options below.

Option 1: Photographic Family Tree

Make a family tree that shows all of the members of your family that you know. The tree should show how everyone is related to you. Put the oldest family members at the top, the next-oldest in the middle, and the youngest at the bottom. Include a photo of as many people as you can. Draw lines between people who have a similar trait and write the trait on the line. The traits can be how they look or act or about their interests and abilities.

Option 2: Flower Guide

There are many types of flowers. They have many more differences than just color. If you look closely, you'll see different petal shapes, different sizes, different arrangements of petals, and different pistils (the part in the middle), along with different shades of petal color.

Make a display of flowers showing how each trait can vary in different flowers. For example, flowers come in a variety of colors. You can show the different colors they come in.

Collect pictures of flowers from magazines, find pictures online, or visit a garden and collect samples (ask permission first).

Flower Guide

color				
shape				
size				
arrangement				
pistil				

Life Science:
Adaptations

Concept

Natural Selection: Sometimes the differences in characteristics between individuals provide advantages in surviving, finding mates, and reproducing.

Lesson Objectives

- Students identify and explain how different adaptations help animals and plants survive in their habitats.
- Students predict how the unique characteristics of an organism can provide an advantage to surviving over others of the same species.

Learning Approach

The learning path in this unit is designed to take students through different phases of learning based on the 5E model. This approach allows students to explore and connect to an idea through relatable activities, to build on prior knowledge and experience, to construct meaning, and to use or apply their understanding of a concept in a creative way.

Teacher Resource Page

Student Pages

Engage

Adaptations

Introduce the Concept

Distribute or display the unit concept page. Read the Spark Question and ask students to think about it. Have students study the animals and plants in the photos and identify the differences of each organism and its habitat. Next, use the text in the Discussion Guide (read it or paraphrase it) to facilitate a conversation that encourages students to think about how people, animals, and plants survive in their own environment. Show short video clips or colored photos of animal and plant behaviors in different habitats. Include examples of mimicry, camouflage, and migration. Ask students to hypothesize how each organism's uniqueness helps it survive. Use Think-Pair-Share, a whole-class discussion, or any other format that suits your class.

Spark Question

How can being different help you survive?

Discussion Guide: Surviving in Your Environment

When the weather outside is cold and windy, how do you keep warm? One way you might get warm is to put on a jacket, a scarf, or a hat. You have now made a change that helps you survive the cold weather in your environment. Plants and animals cannot put on clothes like we can. How can they deal with cold weather or other challenging events that happen in their environment? In this unit, you will learn how plants and animals have changed to survive better in their habitats.

Engage

Adaptations

Adaptations

Plant Adaptation Investigation

You will work in groups of three to investigate how adaptations help living things survive.

What You'll Need

- 2 shallow bowls
- water
- a measuring cup or graduated cylinder
- a celery plant
- a small barrel cactus
- a food scale
- 2 plates (not paper)
- a pencil

What You'll Do

1. Measure ½ cup (120 milliliters) of water into each bowl and record the amount in the first table on the next page.
2. Observe the celery plant and the cactus and weigh them. Record your observations in the second table on the next page. Place the celery plant in one bowl and the cactus in the other.
3. Leave both plants in the water for one hour.
4. Remove each plant. Place each plant on a plate.
5. Measure the water left in each bowl and record the amount in the first table. Calculate how much water each plant absorbed. Discard the water.
6. Weigh each plant and record their weights in the second table. Observe each plant and record your observations.
7. Leave the plants on their plates for three more days. Each day, weigh each plant and record the weight, along with your observations.
8. Then answer the question.

Explore

Adaptations

Data and Observations

Name ______________________________

1. Record the amount of water, the daily weight of each plant, and daily observations.

Amount of water			
Plant	**At the start**	**After 1 hour**	**Difference** (amount absorbed)
celery			
cactus			

Weight			
Date	**Plant**	**Amount**	**Observations**
	celery		
	cactus		
	celery		
	cactus		
	celery		
	cactus		
	celery		
	cactus		
	celery		
	cactus		

Preliminary Explanation

2. Compare the amounts of water used and how each plant looked throughout the investigation. Why do you think they absorbed and held different amounts of water?

____

____

Explore

Adaptations

Arctic Tundra Observation

You will work in groups of three to investigate how adaptations help living things survive.

What You'll Need

- scissors
- animal and plant cards page
- a pencil

What You'll Do

1. Look at the photo below. Read about the Arctic tundra.
2. Then cut out the animal and plant cards on page 48.
3. Read about the animal or plant on each card and look at its photo.
4. Next, discuss with your group which animals you think can live in the Arctic tundra. Sort them into two piles: those that can live in the Arctic tundra and those that can't.
5. Then answer the questions on the next page.

Arctic Tundra

- very cold and windy
- very short summers
- covered in snow most of the year
- flat land with no trees
- dry habitat with little rain

snow-covered plains
floating ice

Adaptations

Preliminary Conclusion

Name ______________________________

1. Which animals and plants can and cannot survive in the Arctic tundra? Draw each animal and plant in one of the boxes. Then explain your answers.

Animals and plants that will survive	Explain.

Animals and plants that will not survive	Explain.

2. Think about the animals that you drew in the first box. What do they have in common?

____

____

____

Explore

Adaptations

Arctic Fox

- is covered in thick white fur
- has furry paws to walk easily on snow and ice
- has short legs, a short nose, and small ears to prevent heat loss
- eats small animals such as mice, birds, hares, and eggs

Polar Bear

- is covered in thick white fur
- spends a lot of time in the water
- has a layer of fat called blubber that keeps it warm
- can get too hot when it runs
- eats meat and plants

Saguaro Cactus

- is covered in spines to protect itself against being eaten
- stores large amounts of water
- can survive in high heat and little rain
- grows very slowly
- can die in freezing temperatures

Pasque Flower

- grows in clumps close to the ground to protect itself against cold winds
- is covered in silky hairs to keep warm
- turns in the direction of the sun
- can grow and make flowers quickly

Harp Seal

- has a layer of fat called blubber that keeps it warm
- swims in the ocean most of the day
- eats fish, shrimp, and krill
- has white fur as a baby
- is born on floating ice

Giraffe

- has light hair with brown or orange patches
- has very long legs and a long neck
- eats leaves from the tops of trees

Surviving Changes

There are many different species of animals and plants on Earth. Some live in the cold Arctic tundra, while others live in a hot desert. Each organism must change or develop special ways to live and survive in its habitat. When a living thing **adapts**, it changes in a way that helps it fit better in a specific environment. Each adaptation depends on the needs of the animal or plant in its environment.

How Do Adaptations Occur?

Adaptations provide advantages in surviving, finding mates, and reproducing. Adaptations in animals and plants happen slowly over time. Imagine that a baby bird is born with a beak that is longer and more curved than the beaks of other birds in its species. Its long, curved beak helps the bird catch more food. Because it can catch more food, it is healthier and stronger than the other birds. It survives longer and has more babies. This bird passes on the **trait** for long, curved beaks to its offspring, who survive longer than other birds, too. Over time, most birds in the species now have long, curved beaks. This is because the traits that help animals and plants survive are passed on to future generations. Traits that are not helpful gradually disappear over time.

A male prairie chicken performs a mating dance.

There are two types of adaptations. Animals and plants can use **behavioral adaptations** to help them survive in their habitat. Behavioral adaptations are things the animal or plant does so its species will survive. For example, a male prairie chicken puffs out its feathers while performing a dance to attract mates. Opossums can slow their heartbeat and lie still to trick predators into thinking they are dead. Coconut trees drop their seeds in or near the ocean so they can float somewhere new to live and grow.

Explain

Adaptations

Physical adaptations can also help living things survive. Physical adaptations are changes that happen to the body of an animal or a plant over time that help the species survive. For example, a squirrel can turn its feet halfway around, making it easy to run from predators in many different directions. A chameleon can change the color of its body to match its surroundings. Underwater plants have flexible stems and leaves to allow the plant to move freely without breaking in strong currents.

Adaptations in Animals

A camel has many adaptations for living in the desert. Most desert habitats are very dry, hot, and sandy. There isn't much water in the desert, so camels drink large amounts of water when they find it. A camel can close its nostrils to protect itself from the sand. It also uses its long eyelashes to shield its eyes from the sun and sand. A camel's thick lips allow it to eat prickly plants without being hurt. Its wide hooves help it walk easily in sand. It stores fat in its humps. It can live off the fat when there is not much food around.

Camels store fat in their humps.

The wings of an owl butterfly trick predators.

An owl butterfly is a tasty treat for birds. However, this butterfly uses an adaptation called **mimicry** to protect itself. Mimicry means acting or looking like something else. It can help a harmless animal look dangerous. An owl butterfly's wings have patterns that look like a pair of owl eyes. Owls eat other birds, so birds get scared off when they see the owl butterfly.

Monarch butterflies use a different adaptation to survive. When the temperature in their habitat gets too cold in the winter, they **migrate** south to warmer temperatures. Other animals such as birds and wildebeests also migrate. Some animals migrate to find food and mates. Groundhogs survive winter by hibernating. When an animal **hibernates**, it falls into a long deep sleep, often for several months. Its body temperature cools and its breathing slows way down. Some kinds of bats and ground squirrels also hibernate to survive cold weather and the lack of food.

Some animals use colors to survive. A poison dart frog's brightly colored skin warns predators to stay away because the frog is poisonous. Male peacocks have brightly colored feathers to attract mates. Other animals use color to **camouflage** themselves. A camouflaged animal blends in with its surroundings so prey and predators can't see it easily. Some owls have feathers the same color as trees. A giraffe's tan hair and orange or brown spots blend into the savanna. An arctic fox's white fur blends into the snow. The fox's prey can't see it coming.

Can you find the camouflaged owl in the tree?

Adaptations in Plants

Cactus plants live in dry, hot deserts where little rain falls. To survive, a cactus will spread its roots far and wide in the ground to collect as much water as possible. When it does rain, some cactus's stems swell to store lots of water. A cactus's stem and leaves have a waxy coating that helps keep in moisture. It is also covered in sharp spines to protect it from animal predators.

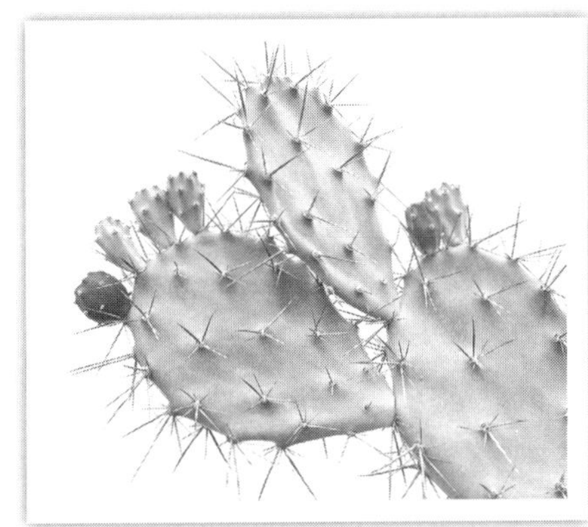

Spines protect this cactus from predators.

Arctic moss uses its adaptations to survive living in the cold Arctic tundra. Arctic moss grows on land and in water. It grows close to the ground where it is warmer and it can be shielded from cold winds. This plant survives harsh winters by going **dormant**. This means the plant is alive but does not grow. It stores nutrients while it is dormant so new leaves can grow in the spring.

Earth is constantly changing, so animals and plants must change, too, in order to survive. Living things that can adapt have the best chance of lasting.

Explain

Adaptations

Concept Vocabulary

adapt:
to change a body part or behavior to help a living thing survive in its habitat

behavioral adaptation:
something a living thing does to survive in its habitat

camouflage:
having colors or markings that allow a living thing to blend in with its surroundings

dormant:
not active for part of the year but still alive

hibernate:
a long deep sleep that helps plants and animals survive difficult conditions

migrate:
to move from one place to another at different times of the year

mimicry:
acting or looking like another living thing

physical adaptation:
a body part or characteristic that helps a living thing survive in its habitat

trait:
a characteristic; a feature; a quality

Notes

Evaluate

Adaptations

Vocabulary Review

Name ____________________

1. Draw a line to match the concept vocabulary term with the correct animal or plant example.

hibernate	Geese fly south for the winter.
mimicry	Tigers have stripes that look like tall grass.
migrate	Snakes often huddle together in dens all winter.
camouflage	A flower smells like something that a fly likes to lay its eggs on.
dormant	Maple trees stop growing in the winter.

Complete the sentences using a concept vocabulary term.

2. Lin had to ____________________ when he moved from China to Sweden.

3. Tropical plants have leaves with pointed tips to help rain drain off them. This is a ____________________ that helps the leaves take in more sunlight.

4. Some plants that live in the Arctic tundra drop seeds quickly in the short warm season. This is a ____________________ that helps the plants reproduce.

5. When a living thing is born with a ____________________, it can be passed on to its offspring.

Evaluate

Adaptations

Concept Comprehension

Name ______________________________

1. Imagine that a group of bugs live on large brown leaves. Some of the bugs are brown and some are green. Which bugs will probably survive? Explain.

2. Think about living things that hibernate and living things that go dormant. What do these adaptations have in common?

   How can you tell if a hedgehog is hibernating?

3. Many plants in the rainforest need sun to live and grow. However, some plants, such as orchids, do not grow tall. Instead, they grow on the tops of tall trees, not in the ground. Is this an example of a behavioral adaptation or a physical adaptation?

   How does this adaptation help the plants that do not grow tall survive?

4. Giraffes use their necks to reach leaves on tall trees. They also swing their necks when fighting for mates. Look at the pictures of two giraffes. Giraffe **A** has a short, thick neck. Giraffe **B** has a long, thin neck. Which one do you think is less likely to go hungry? Which one is more likely to find a mate? Explain your answers.

____

____

____

____

5. Fill in the table to explain how each adaptation helps the animal or plant survive.

Adaptation	**How it helps**
A cactus plant stem can swell.	
Male peacocks have bright and colorful feathers.	
Bears hibernate in the winter.	
An arctic fox has white fur.	

Extend

Adaptations

Describe

Name ______________________

The Pacific walrus lives in the cold waters of the Arctic Ocean. They eat shellfish found on the bottom of the ocean. Walruses depend on floating sheets of ice called ice floes to rest or sleep on between feedings. However, warmer temperatures and more human activities have disturbed the walruses' habitat. This is causing the ice floes to melt and disappear. Walruses are now forced to sleep on land, where baby walruses can be trampled and killed. Mothers now spend more time swimming to their food and less time gathering food and resting,

Describe the cause of the walruses' problem and its effect.

____

____

____

Describe two behavioral adaptations that walruses have made or could make.

____

____

____

Describe two physical adaptations that could help future walruses.

____

____

____

Extend

Adaptations

Imagine

Name ______________________

Imagine that you are a green plant that lives in a rainforest. You grow tall stems and many big leaves to soak up the sun. Your roots do not grow deep into the ground because it rains a lot in your habitat. You make a stinky smell to keep animals from eating you.

Now imagine that a human has moved you to a new desert habitat. Your new home does not rain often, but water can be found deep in the dirt. Everything around you is the color brown. Stinky smells attract the local animals.

Think about what you need to survive. Write at least three adaptations you would need to survive in the desert habitat. Then draw a picture in the box to show what you would look like with the adaptations.

____

____

____

____

____

____

____

____

____

____

____

____

____

____

Plant with adaptations

Adaptations

Project

Choose one of the project options below.

Option 1: Camouflage Butterfly

Make a butterfly that is camouflaged in your classroom. Cut out an outline of a butterfly on a sheet of paper. Then color or glue on items that will help your butterfly blend in. When finished, ask your teacher to hang it in the classroom. See if your classmates can find it.

Option 2: New Animal

Create a new animal that can live in more than one habitat. Research at least two different habitats to find out more about their land, water, weather, temperature, and other plants and animals that live there.

Then think about the new animal you'd like to create. What does it eat? What does it look like? What physical and behavioral adaptations will it need to survive in the habitats you chose? Does it have gills to swim in the ocean or thick fur to live in the cold? Does it sleep in a tight ball for warmth? Does it collect and store food for winter?

Draw a model of your animal and label its body parts and coverings. Write the function of each body part and describe any behavioral adaptations. Give your new animal a unique name.

Life Science:

Organisms in a Changing Environment

Concepts

Interdependent Relationships in Ecosystems: When the environment changes its physical characteristics, temperature, or availability of resources, organisms survive, move, or die. Yet others move into the changed environment.

Biodiversity: Populations live in a variety of habitats, and changes affect the organisms living in them.

Lesson Objectives

- Students explain why organisms survive, move, or die when the environment changes.
- Students investigate why some organisms can survive in an ecosystem while others cannot.

Learning Approach

The learning path in this unit is designed to take students through different phases of learning based on the 5E model. This approach allows students to explore and connect to an idea through relatable activities, to build on prior knowledge and experience, to construct meaning, and to use or apply their understanding of a concept in a creative way.

Teacher Resource Page

Student Pages

Engage

Organisms in a Changing Environment

Introduce the Concept

Distribute or display the unit concept page. Ask students to look at the photos and identify environmental changes. Then read the Spark Question and have them think about it. Next, use the text in the Discussion Guide (read it or paraphrase it) to facilitate a conversation that encourages students to share what they know about environmental changes and the impact they have on the things that live there. Use Think-Pair-Share, a whole-class discussion, or any other format that suits your class.

Spark Question

What do living things do when their home changes?

Discussion Guide: Meeting Needs Where You Live

Have any of you ever lived somewhere else? Where did you live? Why did you move? What did you need that you couldn't get where you lived before? People often live where they can work. Farmers live where there are fields to grow crops. Ship captains live near oceans or large rivers. Animals also need to live where they can meet their needs. Animals that graze on grass need to live in meadows or plains. Plants that need lots of water must live where it rains a lot. But what if it stops raining a lot? What if all of the grass is eaten? Living things must either move somewhere else or change how they meet their needs to stay alive. In this unit, you will learn how and why living things and their surroundings change.

Explore Activity Preparation

In advance: Identify or mark two starting lines at opposite ends of the activity space (Line 1 and Line 2). Identify or mark two circles along the other edges of the activity space (Circle **S** and Circle **D**). Make enough Habitat necklaces for about 80% of the students. Copy and cut apart the Necklace tags on page 64. Attach a string or cord to both sides of each tag. Copy and cut apart enough Survival cards on page 65 for half of your students.

Game play: Divide students evenly into two groups: Rabbits and Habitat Resources (if you have an odd number, have one more Rabbit). Point out the two starting places (Line 1 for Rabbits, Line 2 for Habitat Resources) and the two ending circles (Circle **S** for Survived and Circle **D** for Died). When students are in their starting lines, say, "Hop to it!" At the end of the round, count and record the number of students in each circle. Have Habitat Resources turn in their necklace to you as the remaining Rabbits go back to Line 1. Remove the Shelter necklaces from play; the rest go in a box. Have the new Habitat Resources group choose a necklace from the box. Repeat play. After round 2, remove the Food necklaces. After round 3, remove the Water necklaces. Return to the classroom after round 4. Provide the numbers of Rabbits and Habitat Resources there were at the beginning of each round and at the end of the game. Tell students which Habitat Resource was removed each round.

Organisms in a Changing Environment

Explore

Organisms in a Changing Environment

Rabbit Survival Investigation

You will work with your class to explore how environmental changes can affect animal survival.

What You'll Need

- a large outdoor space
- Habitat necklaces
- Survival cards in a bucket or box

What You'll Do

1. Your teacher will split your class into two groups. Group 1 contains the Rabbits, and Group 2 contains the Habitat Resources. All Rabbits stand on Line 1. Each Habitat Resource receives a Food, Water, Shelter, or Space necklace and stands on Line 2.

2. The game will start when you hear your teacher say, "Hop to it!"
   - Rabbits hop to the box or bucket and take a Survival card to see what habitat resource they need to survive.
   - Rabbits then hop to a classmate on Line 2 who is wearing a Habitat necklace that matches.
   - Once the Rabbit finds a match, both the Rabbit and Habitat Resource hop to the circle labeled **S** where it survives. If a Rabbit cannot find a match, it hops to the circle labeled **D** where it dies. Rabbits that die become Habitat Resources in the next round.
   - At the end of the round, stay in your circles until your teacher tells you where to go to start the next round.

3. Play three more rounds as you did in step 2.

4. Return to your classroom and answer the questions on the next page.

Explore

Organisms in a Changing Environment

Observations

Name ______________________

1. Fill in the table below with the data that your teacher gives you.
Write in the resource or resources that are missing in Rounds 2, 3, and 4:
F = food **W** = water **SH** = shelter **SP** = space

Data at Beginning of Each Round

	Round 1	Round 2	Round 3	Round 4	End of Game
Number of Rabbits					
Number of Habitat Resources					
Missing Resources					

2. What pattern do you see in the number of Rabbits?

____

What pattern do you see in the number of Habitat Resources?

____

What pattern do you see in the missing resources?

____

Preliminary Explanation

3. Why do you think so many Rabbits "died"?

____

____

Habitat Necklace Tags

Organisms in a Changing Environment

Survival Cards

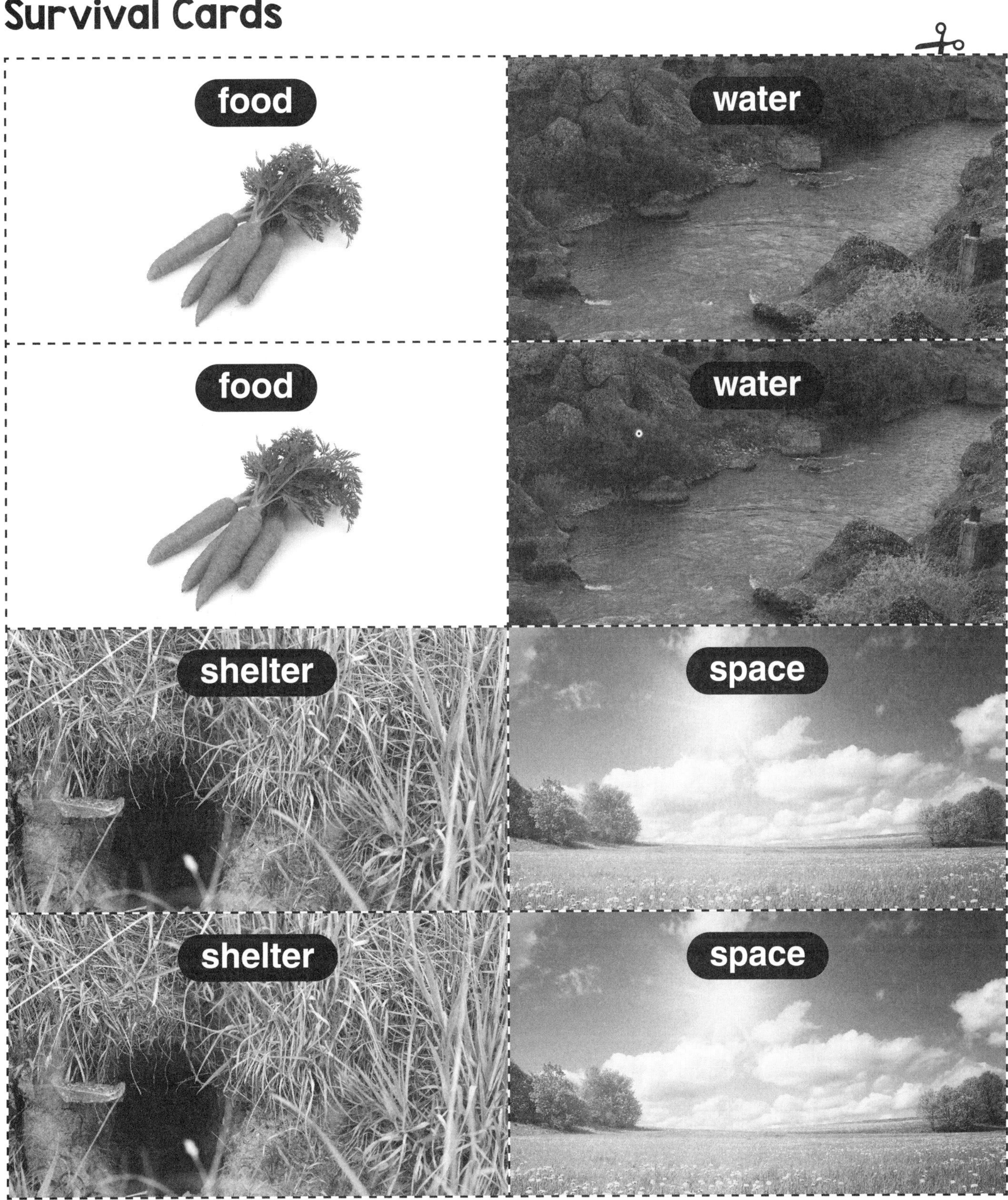

Organisms in a Changing Environment

Change Is Here to Stay

The one thing we can predict about change is that it will never stop. Earth is always changing. Its **physical characteristics** change. The availability of **resources**, such as food, water, and shelter, changes. Some changes are caused by people and some are part of nature. People cut down trees in the forest for lumber. This **deforestation** forces animals out of their homes. People also dump trash and chemicals into the ocean. This is harmful to marine animals and plants. Some changes are caused by weather. **Droughts** leave animals and plants without water, yet too much rainfall can flood **habitats**. Changes in temperature have many impacts on the environment. It melts snow on mountains that becomes our tap water. It also melts the polar ice caps that polar bears live on.

Wherever a change affects an **organism**, the plant or animal may respond with a change of its own. Sometimes its body or behavior adapts. Sometimes it moves to another environment. Sometimes it can't change fast enough and it dies. Sometimes changes in the environment invite new organisms to move there and thrive. Let's look at some examples of different ways that organisms have responded to change.

Rock Pocket Mice

Color is an adaptation that helps animals survive. When animals hide by blending in with the things around them, it is called camouflage. The rock pocket mouse uses this adaptation. When this mouse started living in the desert, its sandy-brown color blended in with the sand and rocks, which camouflaged it. Owls and other animals that eat mice couldn't easily see them, so the rock pocket mice had a good chance of surviving. Then lava from a volcano flowed over part of the desert. The lava cooled into dark rocks. The light-colored mice were not safe on the dark rocks. By chance, a few dark-colored mice were born. The dark-colored mice survived, and the light-colored mice were eaten. More dark-colored mice were born. Now almost all of the rock pocket mice living on the dark rocks are dark-colored. And the mice living in the sandy part of the desert are light-colored.

Iguanas in the Ocean

There are many different **ecosystems** around the world. Ecosystems consist of organisms and nonliving things found together in a single area. In an ecosystem, all organisms depend on each other to survive. One change to an ecosystem impacts all the organisms that live there. The Galápagos (guh-LAH-puh-gohs) Islands are a special ecosystem. Many of the animals that live there are not found anywhere else. One such animal is a lizard called the Galápagos iguana. All lizards are land animals except for these iguanas. They swim into the ocean to eat tiny water plants called algae. Then the iguanas return to land to warm up in the sun. In years when the ocean is warmer, there are fewer algae to eat. When iguanas eat less, their bones shrink. Their smaller bodies warm up in the sun more quickly so they can make more trips to feed in the water. When the ocean becomes colder again, the iguanas grow larger.

Brown Tree Snakes

Without knowing it, people changed the ecosystem on the island of Guam (gwahm). Brown tree snakes slipped in around the year 1950. They were hiding in the wheels of military planes and boats. Now there are more than two million brown

Organisms in a Changing Environment

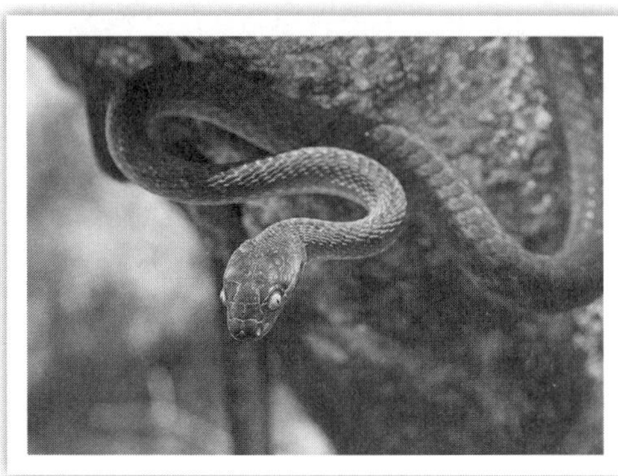

snakes on Guam. The snakes have caused big changes in the island's ecosystem. There used to be many forest birds, but the snakes ate them. Now nearly all the birds are gone, and some species of birds are **extinct**. Because there are fewer birds to eat spiders, there are many more spiders. There are not enough birds to help spread seeds, so fewer new trees and plants grow in the forest. Scientists are working to find ways to get rid of the snakes without harming other parts of the ecosystem.

Paperbark Trees

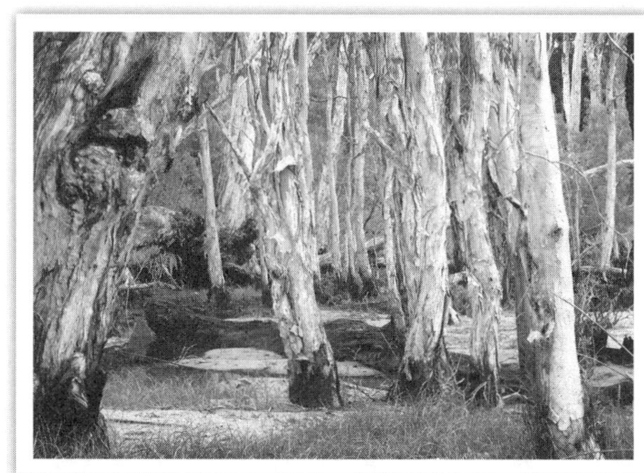

People brought paperbark trees from Australia to Florida in the 1880s. They hoped the trees could help dry out swampy land. But the paperbark trees took over. They blocked out light and made it impossible for Florida's **native** plants to grow. Without the native plants, many animal and insect species couldn't survive. Unfortunately, very few animal species can live in the paperbark tree's habitat.

Another problem is that the trees survive Florida's wildfires but Florida's native plants do not. So there are fewer native plants and more paperbark trees. Scientists know that this tree has changed the ecosystem in Florida. They are working to control the spread of these trees.

Changes to an ecosystem force plants and animals to adapt. However, some changes, such as fires, make it impossible for organisms to survive, even with their adaptations. People often impact the environment, even when they are trying to improve it. They must make careful decisions. But some changes cannot be avoided, as Earth is always changing. Organisms will change, as well, if they are to survive.

Explain

Organisms in a Changing Environment

Concept Vocabulary

deforestation:
removing many trees from a forest and then using the land for something else

drought:
a long period of time with no rain or snow

ecosystem:
all living and nonliving things that share an environment

extinct:
no longer existing; when a whole species dies out

habitat:
a place where plants and animals naturally live

native:
originally from a particular place

organism:
a living thing

physical characteristic:
something about a thing or a place that you find out with your senses

resource:
a thing that is useful

Notes

Evaluate

Organisms in a Changing Environment

Vocabulary Review

Name ______________________________

1. Look at the photo. Write three **physical characteristics** about the animal and the habitat.

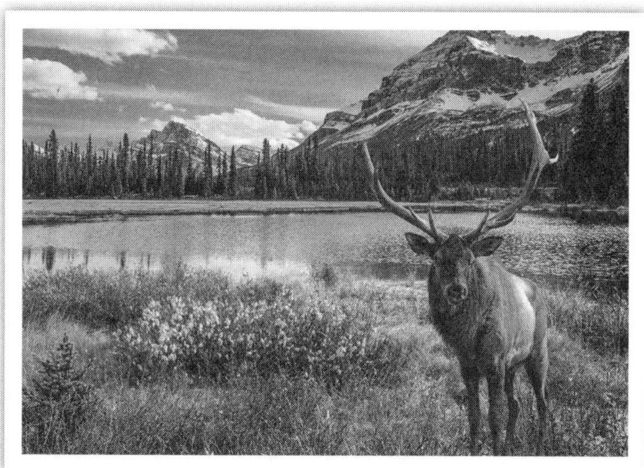

animal	habitat
________________	________________
________________	________________
________________	________________

2. Draw an example for each term. Then explain your picture.

deforestation	native
In my picture, ________________	In my picture, ________________
________________	________________
________________.	________________.

3. Circle the example of an **organism**.

a chair   an insect   the wind

4. Complete the rhyme using terms from the Concept Vocabulary page.

A ____________________, where a living thing lives,

Provides ____________________ needed to grow and have kids.

If there is a ____________________, there is no rain for a time,

Or maybe it floods, or temperatures climb!

____________________ change in more ways than you think,

So living things change or become ____________________.

5. A **haiku** is a short poem. It has only three lines. The first and last lines have 5 syllables. The second line has 7 syllables. This is an example of a haiku:

Resources

Natural from Earth
Others are made by people
These things are useful

Choose a concept vocabulary term and write a haiku about it. Then draw a picture.

concept vocabulary term:

____

____

____

____

Organisms in a Changing Environment

Concept Comprehension

Name ____________________

1. Which photo shows a change that caused a problem in the environment?

Explain the problem. ____________________

____

____

2. Draw a picture in each box to show how brown tree snakes affected the numbers of birds and spiders.

Birds	Spiders

Explain your drawings. ____________________

____

____

Scientists have been keeping track of where birds live in North America. They noticed that many birds are moving north. They made a graph to show how far north they now live. Look at the graph and answer questions 3 through 6.

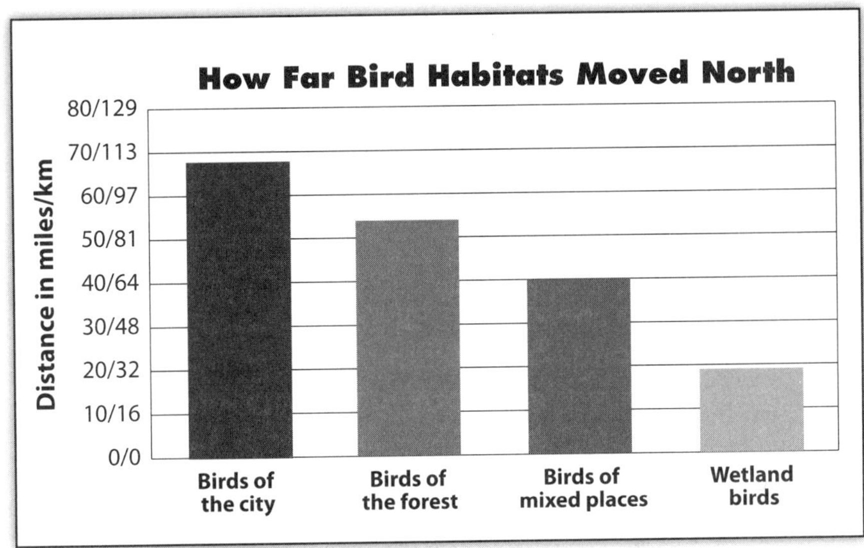

3. Which types of birds moved the farthest?

Name one kind of change these birds may have faced that made them move.

___

4. The birds that were tracked changed their ______.

physical characteristics   behavior

5. Why do you think all types of birds moved north instead of another direction?

___

___

6. Look at the photo. Which type of bird from the graph do you think this is?

___

Explain why you think so.

___

___

___

Extend

Organisms in a Changing Environment

Solve

Name ______________________________

Imagine that a drought is changing a forest habitat. Think about how the resources in that forest may change. Now imagine that you are one of the plants or animals that live in that forest. How might you be affected by the change? What can you do to respond to it? You may do something different, or your species may develop a physical adaptation over time.

Write a journal entry as the plant or animal you chose. Describe how the change will affect you and what you hope to do so that you or your offspring survive it.

Organisms in a Changing Environment

Debate

Name ____________________

Your friend says, "Ecosystems should not change! Let's find a way to keep them the same! Changes only cause problems!" Do you agree or disagree? State your opinion and explain it. Support your opinion with facts.

Extend

Organisms in a Changing Environment

Project

Choose one of the project options below.

Option 1: Extinct Animal Science Fair Display

Make a presentation for the science fair about an extinct animal. Choose an extinct animal and tell all about it. Include information such as its name, how long it lived on Earth, when it became extinct, why or how it became extinct, the habitat it lived in, resources it needed to survive, and any other interesting facts. Also include pictures of your animal. Write down any online clips, books, or Internet sources that you used.

Tasmanian tiger

Glyptodon

Woolly mammoth

Dodo bird

Option 2: Ecosystem Change Timeline

Find out about the history of the environment or ecosystem around you. You might explore insects, animals, trees, and plants, as well as adaptations they may have. If possible, include what this area was like 50 years ago. Think about questions such as "What has changed?" and "Have any organisms survived, moved, or died?" Create an illustrated timeline of each change with a description of the change.

Paul R. Jones / Shutterstock.com

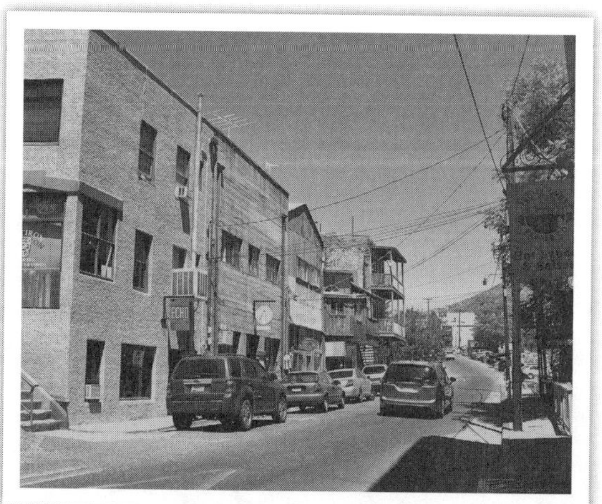
Paul R. Jones / Shutterstock.com

Life Science:
Group Social Behavior

Concept

Social Interactions and Group Behavior: Being part of a group helps animals obtain food, defend themselves, and cope with changes. Groups have different functions and size.

Lesson Objectives

- Students investigate and discover why animals form groups to survive.
- Students determine advantages and disadvantages of living in a group.

Learning Approach

The learning path in this unit is designed to take students through different phases of learning based on the 5E model. This approach allows students to explore and connect to an idea through relatable activities, to build on prior knowledge and experience, to construct meaning, and to use or apply their understanding of a concept in a creative way.

Teacher Resource Page

Student Pages

Engage

Group Social Behavior

Introduce the Concept

Distribute or display the unit concept page. Read the Spark Question and ask students to think about it. Ask students to look at the photos to hypothesize what each group of animals is doing together and how working together helps them. Next, use the text in the Discussion Guide (read it or paraphrase it) to facilitate a conversation that encourages students to explain why they think animals live in groups. Use Think-Pair-Share, a whole-class discussion, or any other format that suits your class.

Spark Question

Why do many living things live in groups?

Discussion Guide: Helping Each Other

Whom do you live with? Why do you live with others? Do you need help from others to get all the things you need to live and grow? For example, where do you go when you are hungry? Who prepares your food at home, at school, or at a restaurant? You can go to a market where fresh fruits and vegetables are already grown, harvested, and ready for you to eat. Without help from restaurants, stores, and farmers, people would have to find and grow their own foods. Can you think of other ways that people help each other? Many animals, including humans, live in groups to survive. Group sizes can vary, and they can live together for many different reasons. In this unit, you will learn just how important groups are.

Explore Activity Preparation

Reproduce the data table on page 81 for yourself. Find a playground or field where students can safely run. Outline the area if needed. Mark off a small rectangle with tape, cones, or rope on each end of the play area. This is each team's home. For each round, group students as either Prey or Predator. Designate a flag color for each role. Give a stuffed animal to the Prey team. Change the number of students per group for each round (see chart at the right).

Suggested Grouping Plan

	Prey	Predators
Round 1	50%	50%
Round 2	75%	25%
Round 3	15%	85%
Round 4	25%	75%
Round 5	85%	15%

Point out each team's home and have students go to their team's side. Also point out the place to go when they are tagged out. Make sure all students understand the rules and the goal. Be sure the students have their flags attached at the start of each round. Start each round and set a timer for 5 minutes. Record the number of students on each team for each round, as well as each round's result, on the data table.

Engage

Group Social Behavior

Group Social Behavior

Capture the Prey

You will work with your class to investigate the benefits of living in a group.

What You'll Need

- a large outdoor space
- tape
- two different-colored flags (bandana, small towel, or piece of cloth) for each student

What You'll Do

1. Your class will go outside to the play area. Your teacher will split your class into two teams: Prey and Predators. Each round will have a different number of students on each team.
2. Tuck or tape one end of the correctly colored flag on one side of your waist.
3. Your teacher will show you where each team will start. The Prey team will have a stuffed animal that the Predators will try to take away. Your teacher will tell you when to start. Here are the game rules:
   - Predators have 5 minutes to try to grab the stuffed animal prey and bring it to their home without having their flags taken away.
   - Prey must protect the stuffed animal but must also not be "eaten" (have their flags taken away).
   - Players on both teams try to grab the other team's players' flags to tag them out. If a Prey or a Predator loses his or her flag, that player must sit out and watch the rest of the round.
   - The round ends in one of three ways: 1) when the Predators successfully take the stuffed prey to their home, 2) when all members of a team have their flags taken away, or 3) when 5 minutes are up.
4. After 5 rounds, go back to your classroom and answer the questions on the next page.

Explore

Group Social Behavior

Data

Name ______________________________

1. Complete the data table with information from your teacher.

Round	Number of Prey	Number of Predators	Did the predators capture the stuffed prey?
1			yes no
2			yes no
3			yes no
4			yes no
5			yes no

Preliminary Explanation

2. What were some reasons the Predators were able to catch the stuffed prey?

____

____

3. What were some reasons the stuffed prey survived?

____

____

4. How did the size of the team affect how successful the team was?

____

____

5. Why do you think some animals live in groups?

____

____

Group Social Behavior

Better Together

Chimpanzees groom each other. Fish stay safe by swimming in large groups called **schools**. Humans support each other in families. These are a few examples of animal **group behaviors**. The behaviors help animals meet each other's needs.

Chimpanzees live, eat, and play together. Grooming others is a sign of love and trust.

Many species of animals live in groups, including us humans. Groups can be as small as two members or as large as thousands of members. Groups live together for different reasons. Most animals live in groups to help obtain food, defend themselves, and adapt to changes.

Gathering Food

Living in groups has many **advantages**. One advantage is that it is easier to find food. Dolphins are social animals that work together to hunt fish and squid. Dolphins live in a group called a **pod**. A pod of dolphins will **herd** fish into small groups and trap them in shallow water or against a sandbar. Then the dolphins will take turns eating the trapped fish. Members of a pod also work together to keep their young safe. When they swim, younger dolphins are kept in the middle of the pod for protection.

Dolphins live in groups called pods.

Being part of a group also allows smaller predators to hunt and eat larger-sized prey. Wolves are a perfect example of this. Wolves live together in family groups called **packs**. A wolf pack usually has between 6 and 12 members. All the members of the pack work together to take care of the young pups, protect their territory, and hunt for food. Wolves like to eat large animals such as bison. But bison weigh up to 15 times what a wolf weighs, so hunting in a group is important. When the hunt is a success, the meat is shared with all the wolves in the pack.

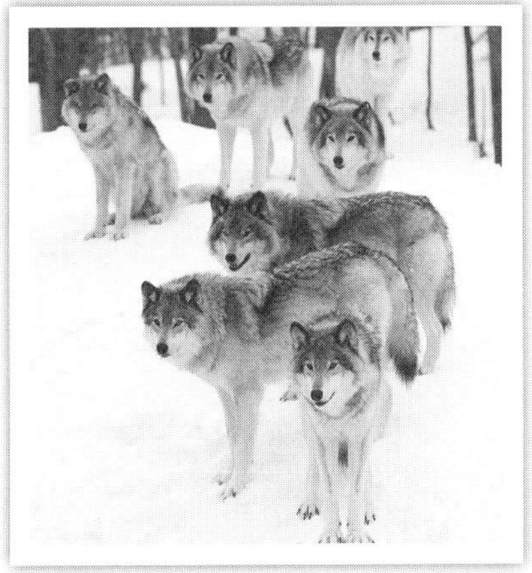

Wolves hunt in packs.

Defending Themselves

There is safety in numbers. This is why many animals, like meerkats, live in groups. A group of meerkats is called a **mob**. A mob of meerkats can have 20 to 50 members. Each member takes turns doing a job that helps the group. One important job is watching out for predators. One or more meerkats in the mob will find a high place such as a tall rock, and stand up on its back legs to watch for predators. This allows other members to dig tunnels, babysit the young, or eat a meal in peace. When the guard spots a predator, it lets out a warning bark and the other meerkats quickly take shelter in their tunnels. Sometimes, predators find meerkats in an open area. If this happens, the mob stands close together on their back feet while they hiss and bare their teeth. This tricks the predator into thinking the meerkats are one big animal.

Meerkats stand on their back feet to look out for predators.

Penguins live in large groups called a **waddle**. Waddles of emperor penguins live in the Antarctic, where harsh temperatures can dip well below freezing. To stay warm in such extreme weather, penguins **huddle** together. The penguins in the middle of the huddle warm up as the others protect them from the cold winds. Once a penguin in the

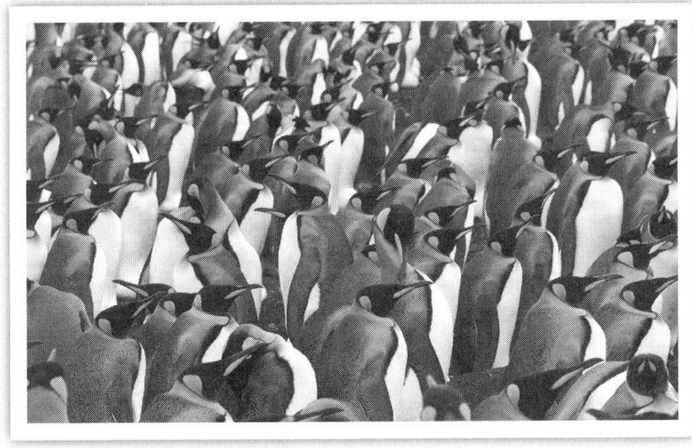

Penguins huddle together to keep warm.

Group Social Behavior

middle is warm enough, it moves to the outer edge of the group so others get a turn to warm up. Penguins also team up to help care for all the young. About two months after the babies have hatched, they are able to stand on the frozen ground. The youngsters are kept safe in nurseries while the parents bring home more fish.

Working Together

Ants live in underground nests in a group called a **colony**, which can have millions of members. Each member of the colony has a specific job. Some worker ants protect the queen and the babies. Other worker ants find food and bring it back to the nest. During a flood or a heavy rainstorm, their nests can fill up with water. The ants are forced to leave or drown. Fire ants lock legs to create a raft. They use it to float to a safe place. They can also create a bridge between parts of a plant. They can use this to reach high places or cross from one branch to another.

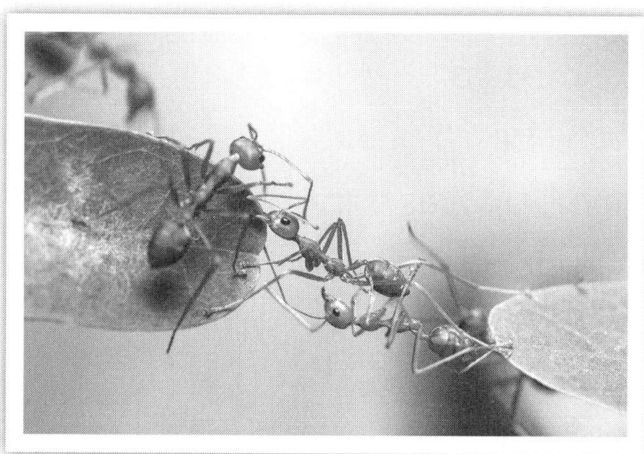

Ants climb on top of each other and lock legs to create a bridge.

Disadvantages of Living in a Group

Although there are many advantages to living in a group, there are also **disadvantages**. When many animals live in a group, disease spreads easily from one member to another. Predators can spot a large group of animals more easily than they can spot a single animal. Also, there is more competition for group members to find a mate.

Male elk compete for mates.

Living in groups isn't perfect. But it solves many challenges that animals face in finding food, staying safe, and dealing with their environment.

Explain

Group Social Behavior

Concept Vocabulary

advantage:
something that helps you succeed

colony:
a group of ants

disadvantage:
something that does not help you succeed

group behaviors:
what animals do with other animals for the same purpose

herd:
to make animals move together

huddle:
to crowd together in a tight group

mob:
a group of meerkats

pack:
a group of wolves

pod:
a group of dolphins

school:
a group of fish

waddle:
a group of penguins

Notes

Evaluate

Group Social Behavior

Vocabulary Review

Name ______________________________

1. Draw a picture that shows an example of each group of animals.

mob	waddle
pod	pack
colony	school

2. Which sentence describes a **group behavior**?

   - ○ In the fall, brown bears eat up to 90 pounds of food a day to prepare to hibernate.
   - ○ Lions hunt together to catch prey that are often bigger than they are.
   - ○ A leopard hides in tall grass before it lunges at its prey.

3. Which photo shows people in a **huddle**?

○

○

4. Complete the paragraph using concept vocabulary terms.

Jalen was nervous as he waited outside the ballpark. Today he was going to try out for Little League. He looked at the other players who were trying out. Many were taller and stronger-looking. This would give them an ________________. But there was no turning back now. The coach opened the door and began to ________________ all the athletes into the stands. It was time to start the tryouts. Jalen tried not to think about how his skinny arms and short legs put him at a ________________. Jalen took a deep breath as he got ready to fight for a spot on a team.

Evaluate

Group Social Behavior

Concept Comprehension

Name ______________________________

1. Fill in the table with three reasons animals live in groups. Then give an example of each.

Reason animals live in groups	Example

2. Humans live in groups, too. Give two examples of how humans work together to survive.

____

____

3. Animal groups can vary in size. Think about one need that groups have. Compare how life would be for a small group and a large group.

____

____

____

____

4. Fill in the boxes below with a cause or effect of group behaviors.

Cause: Rain floods an ant colony nest.

Effect:

Cause: Cold winds blow in the Antarctic where penguins live.

Effect:

Cause:

Effect: The whole group of meerkats quickly hides in its tunnels for safety.

5. Read the statements in the boxes below. Write on the line above each one whether it is an **advantage** or a **disadvantage** of living in groups. Then write another advantage and disadvantage of living in groups in the bottom boxes.

______________________	______________________
Disease spreads faster in groups.	There are more members to help take care of the young.

Group Social Behavior

Justify

Name

Imagine that you have a friend who wants to live alone on an island. There are no markets to shop at or technology to use on the island. Write a letter to your friend. Justify why you think your friend should not live alone. Give reasons why living in a group would help him or her survive on the island.

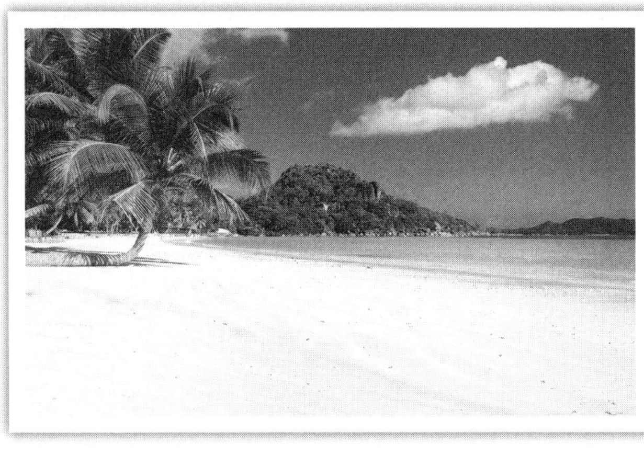

Group Social Behavior

Apply

Name________________________________

Jaguars are solitary animals. This means they live alone. Jaguars mostly live in rainforests and woods, but they can also be found in deserts. Their powerful jaws help them eat turtles, frogs, fish, deer, and even alligators. Jaguars do not like other jaguars near their homes. They will mark their territories with urine and claw marks on trees. Use what you know about living in groups to answer the questions.

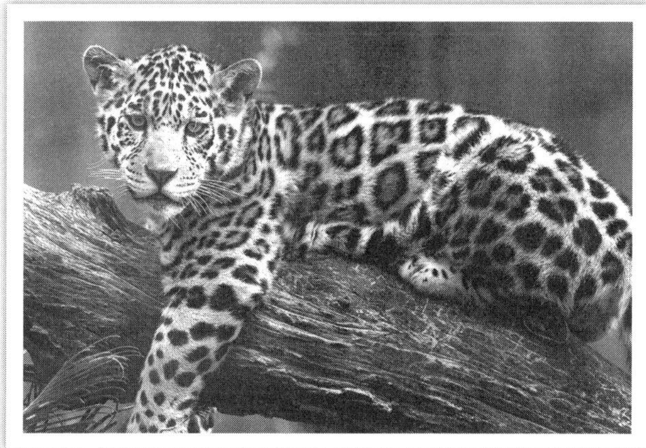

1. What are some advantages of the jaguar living alone?

____

____

____

2. What are some disadvantages of the jaguar living alone?

____

____

____

3. A jaguar will work together with another jaguar only for a special occasion. When do you think jaguars need to work with others? Why is it important for their survival?

____

____

____

____

Extend

Group Social Behavior

Project

Choose one of the project options below.

Option 1: Animal Groups Video

Make a video or a display using video clips or photos showing different animals or humans living in groups. Include descriptions of the group behaviors and how the behaviors help the group survive. Write down the source of any online clips or pictures you use.

Option 2: Ant Farm

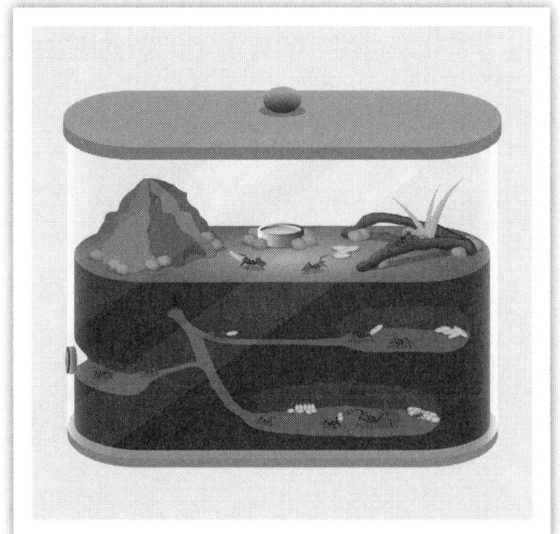

Set up an ant farm. Find two jars with lids—one big jar and another smaller jar that fits inside the big jar. Fill the smaller jar with dirt and close the lid. Place the smaller jar inside the big jar. Fill the space in between the two jars with soil and dirt. Leave a little space at the top. With the help of an adult, find some ants. Put on gloves and use a spoon to scoop up the ants and put them into the big jar. Screw on the lid. Have an adult poke holes in the lid to give air to the ants. Every few days, feed your ants small drops of honey, jam, or a piece of fruit on top of the small jar inside the big jar. Also place a wet cotton ball next to your food, or gently squeeze the water on the dirt. When you aren't observing the ants, cover your ant farm with a dark cloth. This makes the ants think they are tunneling underground.

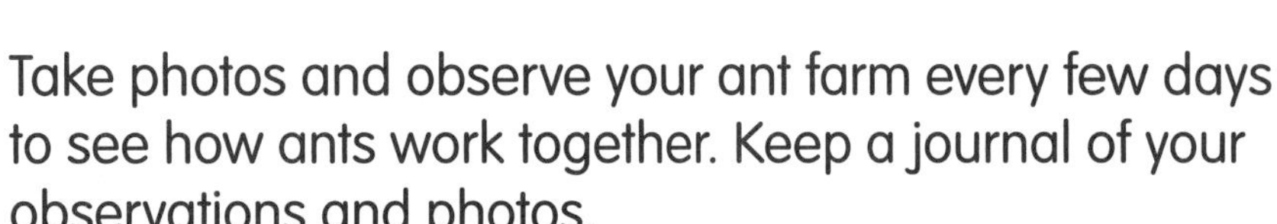

Take photos and observe your ant farm every few days to see how ants work together. Keep a journal of your observations and photos.

Life Science:
Fossils of Ancestors

Concept

Evidence of Common Ancestry: Some kinds of plants and animals that once lived on Earth are no longer found anywhere. Fossils provide evidence about the types of organisms that lived long ago and also about the nature of their environments.

Lesson Objectives

- Students describe fossils and how they form.
- Students discover information that scientists can learn from fossils.

Learning Approach

The learning path in this unit is designed to take students through different phases of learning based on the 5E model. This approach allows students to explore and connect to an idea through relatable activities, to build on prior knowledge and experience, to construct meaning, and to use or apply their understanding of a concept in a creative way.

Teacher Resource Page

Student Pages

Engage

Fossils of Ancestors

Introduce the Concept

Read the Spark Question and ask students to think about it. Distribute or display the unit concept page. Have students study the different fossil images in the photos. Next, use the text in the Discussion Guide (read it or paraphrase it) to facilitate a conversation that encourages students to share what they know about living things that came before us. Use Think-Pair-Share, a whole-class discussion, or any other format that suits your class.

Spark Question

How do we know that dinosaurs existed?

Discussion Guide: Finding Clues to Past Life

Detectives use clues to solve mysteries. What are some examples of clues that a detective might use? What do those clues tell him or her? You might even find clues to mysteries in your own house. Let's say you went into your kitchen to get a cookie, but the jar is empty! You know that your parents just filled it. You look around for clues, and you see small footprints on the floor from the doorway to the cookie jar. What does this clue tell you? Who could have made those footprints? What do you think happened to the cookies?

Paleontologists are scientists who solve mysteries about life that lived long ago. Many plants and animals lived on this planet before humans came along. While most died without a trace, some of them did leave traces that we can use as clues about their lives. What are some animals that lived on Earth long ago? What clues did paleontologists find that proved these animals existed? In this unit, you will learn how we solve mysteries of life long ago.

Explore Activity Preparation

Mix plaster of Paris with water according to the package directions just before starting the activity. Pour the plaster into shallow plastic disposable trays, one for each pair of students.

After students unmold their fossils, collect the bowls or dishes of objects that each pair used. Place them in a central location in the classroom before students meet with another pair of students.

Fossils of Ancestors

Busara / Shutterstock.com

Explore

Fossils of Ancestors

Fossil Investigation

You will work in pairs to model how fossils are made and used.

What You'll Need

- small plastic or metal objects
- a spoon
- petroleum jelly
- paper towels
- a tray of plaster
- an empty bowl or dish
- a piece of masking tape
- a marker
- blank paper
- a pencil

What You'll Do

1. Choose several objects. Coat the first object with petroleum jelly. Set the coated object gently into the plaster. You should still see part of the object above the plaster. Repeat with the remaining objects.
2. Let the plaster dry overnight.
3. The next day, write your names on the masking tape and place the tape on the bottom of your bowl or dish. Carefully remove the objects from the dried plaster and place them in the bowl or dish.
4. Observe the dried plaster and record your observations on the next page.
5. Meet with another pair of students and trade plaster trays. Examine the fossils left in the plaster. Draw each one on the blank paper and write what you think your classmates used to make it.
6. Look at all of the bowls or dishes of objects used to make the plaster fossils. Try to figure out which set of objects was used by the other pair of students. When you find it, check the names on the bottom of the bowl or dish.
7. Then answer the questions on the next page.

Explore

Fossils of Ancestors

Observations

Name ______________________________

1. What did you observe in the plaster when you removed the objects?

____

Preliminary Explanation

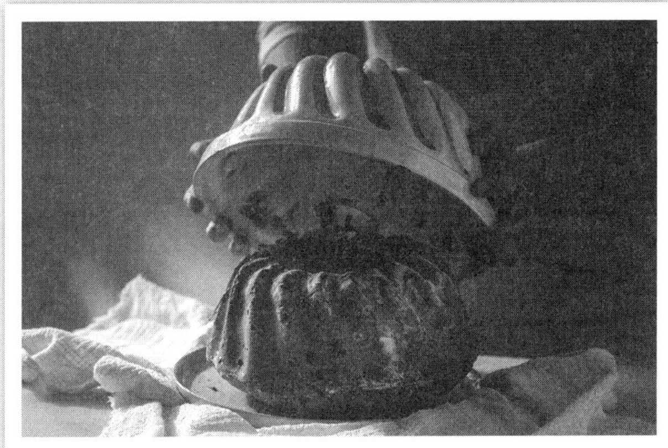

2. A mold is a hole in the shape of something. A cast is made when you put something in that hole to form the shape. In the photo, the cake pan is the mold and the cake is the cast. Do you think your object fossils are examples of a mold or a cast?

____

3. How many objects could you correctly identify from the other pair's plaster tray? How could you figure out what made each fossil?

____

What information about the objects could you <u>not</u> figure out?

____

4. Scientists examine fossils made in rocks. How do you think the activity you just did is similar to what scientists do?

____

____

How is it different? ____

____

____

Explain

Fossils of Ancestors

Clues from Long Ago

You've heard of dinosaurs but you've never seen a live one, right? Humans have never seen them alive. Dinosaurs no longer exist. We don't have any photos of them roaming around. So how do we even know about them?

For a long time, people have found **fossils** in the ground. There are several types of fossils. One type of fossil is a hard body part, such as a bone, shell, or tooth, from long ago. It could also be in the shape of a body part pressed into a rock. Some fossils looked like things (or parts of things) that are alive today, but others didn't look like anything that is currently alive on Earth. Scientists realized that living things have changed over time. Many of these fossils showed us what living things were like in the past. Fossils are like natural photographs of what used to live on Earth.

How Fossils Form

Have you ever left a toy outside for a long time? When you finally try to pick it up, you find that wind and rain have slowly covered it with a layer of dirt. If it's been there for months or more, it may even have sunk a little into the dirt. You might have to pry it loose.

cast

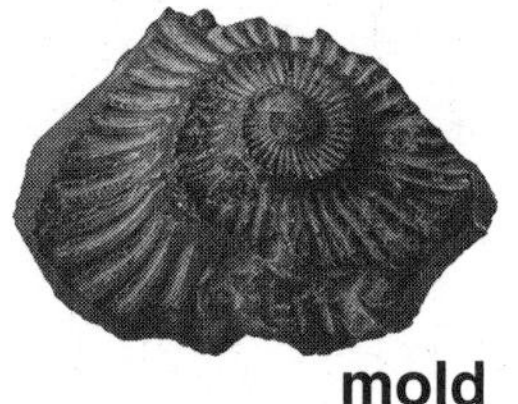

mold

This is similar to the way many fossils form. A living thing dies, and its body is covered by layers of **sediment**. The body usually **decays** but leaves a hole where it was. This hole is called a **mold**. Sometimes that hole gets filled in by minerals (bits of nonliving matter) that form in the exact shape of the hole left behind by the living thing. This is called a **cast**. Over millions of years, heavy layers of sediment pile up and form into **sedimentary rock**. Many of the fossils seen in museums were formed this way.

Sometimes the original body parts are found, rather than molds and casts. One example of this is when an insect gets caught in tree resin, a soft, sticky liquid that flows from some trees. There is no air around the insect. It dies, but it doesn't decay. Eventually, the tree dies and falls into a swamp. The tree is slowly covered by sediment. Millions of years pass. The resin turns into a clear yellow fossil called amber. The tiny insect can still be seen inside!

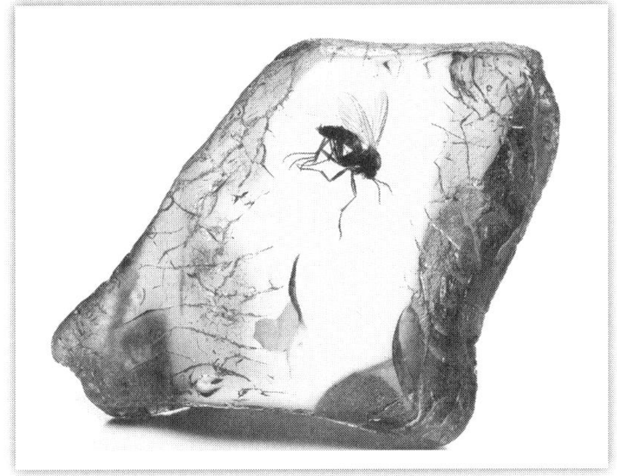

An insect caught in amber

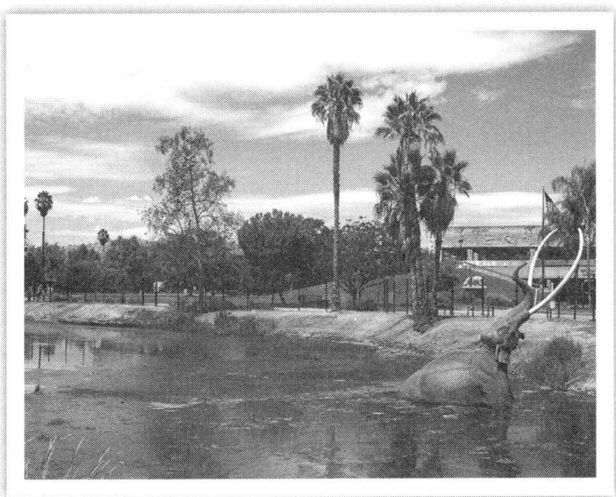

Model of a mammoth trapped in the La Brea Tar Pits

Another example of finding actual body parts is at the La Brea Tar Pits in the city of Los Angeles. That's where **paleontologists** have found the bones of saber-toothed cats, Columbian mammoths, and many old and modern animals stuck in pits of sticky liquid. The extinct animals were trapped in pools of black goo called asphalt at least 55,000 years ago. Thousands of fossils have been found in the tar pits, and more are still being **excavated** today!

Information from Fossils

Not all fossils are plant and animal body parts. **Trace fossils** are made from things such as footprints, droppings, or nests. Trace fossils can tell scientists how animals moved and lived. For example, footprints of dinosaurs have shown us how they walked. They can tell how large a dinosaur was by how far apart its steps were.

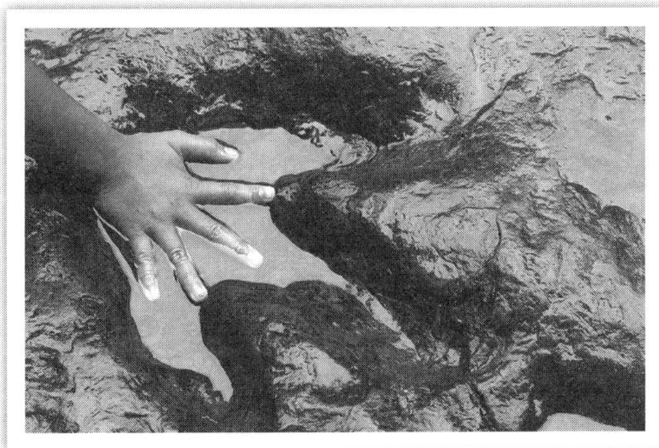

Comparing a human hand to a dinosaur footprint helps scientists figure out how large the animal was.

Fossils of Ancestors

Think about a parent walking with a young child, two or three years old, or walking a dog. The child or dog must take several steps for every single step the parent takes. Think about the difference in size of the parent and the child or dog. The larger an animal is, the longer its steps are. If there is more than one set, footprints might even show us that a type of dinosaur traveled in pairs or groups.

How Scientists Find Fossils

Fossils are found when rock is dug up or when rock naturally wears away and reveals buried layers. The place where a fossil is found can reveal interesting information. Over time, fossils get buried deeper and deeper. Fossils found in the upper layers of Earth's crust often mean the organism lived and died more recently. The fossils found in deeper layers are usually organisms from longer ago. Most of them are **extinct**. Dinosaur fossils have been found only in rock layers that are at least 65 million years old. That is most likely when the last of the dinosaurs died out.

Older animals appear in lower layers.

We use **evidence** to figure things out all the time. If you see a dirty plate and fork in the sink, you know that someone probably ate something. If you see a wet umbrella near the door, you know that it has probably been raining outside. Fossils are evidence of past lives. They prove that Earth's history once included these creatures, even if they no longer exist. They remind us to learn all we can about the organisms that are here now and to do what we can to keep them around.

Tusks of a mammoth at a dig site

Explain

Fossils of Ancestors

Concept Vocabulary

cast:
a fossil made by nonliving matter that fills a mold fossil

decay:
to break down or rot

evidence:
proof that shows something happened

excavate:
to dig out and remove fossils

extinct:
no longer existing; when a species dies out

fossil:
a body part or a mark left behind by a plant or an animal that lived long ago

mold:
a fossil showing the space left by a living thing that has rotted away

paleontologist:
a scientist who uses fossils to study living things of the past

sediment:
soil or sand that forms layers of land

sedimentary rock:
rock formed when layers of soil and sand have been pressed together over time

trace fossil:
a fossil of an animal footprint or track

Notes

Evaluate

Fossils of Ancestors

Vocabulary Review

Name ______________________________

1. Describe four types of fossils. Then write each letter next to its photo.

   a. ______________________________

   b. ______________________________

   c. ______________________________

   d. ______________________________

_____ 

Tangopaso

_____ 

_____ 

_____ 

2. Look at the diagram. Label the **fossil** and the **sediment**.

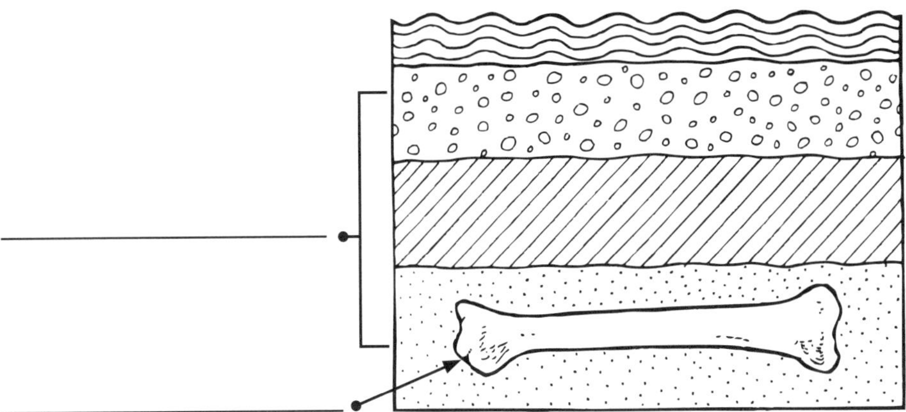

3. Complete the paragraph using concept vocabulary terms.

Robert hadn't planned to be a ______________________. He grew up in northern Alaska. It's so cold there that the ground stays frozen all year long. But the rivers and streams melt in the short summer. One summer, Robert was looking for gold in a riverbed. Out of the corner of his eye, he saw something odd. He looked over at the ______________________. In one of the layers, he spotted a strange-looking bone. He ran home and brought his mother back. Together, they carefully ______________________ the bone. It turned out to be a long mammoth tusk! Unfortunately, the rest of the mammoth's body had ______________________. But Robert's first piece of ______________________ proved that he and mammoths, which are ______________________, had wandered the same land.

Evaluate

Fossils of Ancestors

Concept Comprehension

Name ______________________________

1. What is the difference between a dead plant and an extinct plant?

____

____

____

2. What are two liquids in which you might find fossils containing body parts of animals?

______________________________ ______________________________

3. Write three examples of information that fossils can tell us about extinct animals.

____

____

What can an amber fossil tell scientists that a trace fossil cannot tell them?

____

____

____

4. Paleontologists have found dinosaur skulls with sharp teeth and others with flat teeth. What do you think this difference could tell scientists?

____

____

____

5. Write **true** or **false**.

a. Fossils form quickly and are very common. ____________

b. Sand and soil are two kinds of sediment. ____________

c. A dead plant will turn into a fossil within ten years. ____________

d. Minerals take the place of bones in cast fossils. ____________

e. Dinosaurs went extinct about 65 million years ago. ____________

f. Shells, teeth, and bones decay in sediment. ____________

g. Humans and dinosaurs lived during the same time. ____________

h. Minerals are nonliving things. ____________

Use the diagram to help you answer questions 6 and 7.

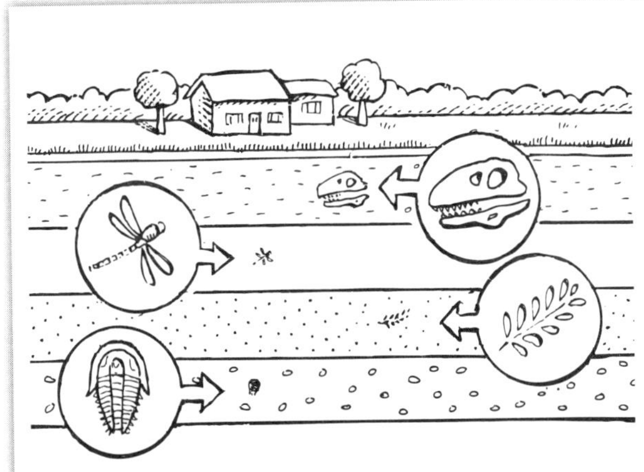

6. Are the oldest fossils likely to be in the top layer, middle layer, or bottom layer? Explain why.

____

____

____

____

____

7. If paleontologists found a fossil in the middle layer that was 2 million years old, would they think that Earth was more or less than 2 million years old? Why?

____

____

____

____

Extend

Fossils of Ancestors

Imagine

Name ______________________

Imagine that you are a shell fossil. You were once part of a live sea animal that is now extinct. You have just been found by a paleontologist. Tell the story of your life and how you came to be where the scientist dug you up.

Extend

Fossils of Ancestors

Reflect

Name ____________________

Not all paleontologists study dinosaurs. Some may study plants, cats, turtles, bacteria, sponges, sea stars, worms, and many other forms of life. If you were a paleontologist, write what life-form or life-forms you would like to study and explain why.

Extend

Fossils of Ancestors

Project

Choose one of the project options below.

Option 1: Our Local Fossil

In the United States, many states have chosen a state fossil. Usually they choose a fossil of something that lived in that region long ago. Imagine that your city, town, or school is having a contest to choose a fossil to represent where you live. Find out what plants and animals lived in your area long ago. Choose one that you think would make a good city, town, or school fossil. Draw the fossil and write about it. Explain to the contest judges why this is a good fossil choice.

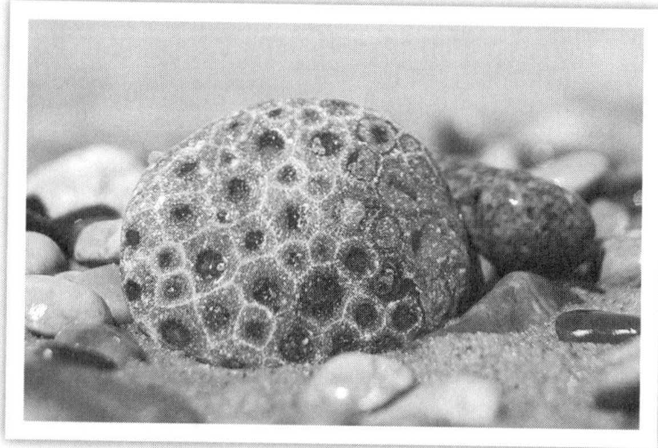

Michigan's Petoskey stone is one of two state fossils. The "stones" are from a coral reef. The reef's coral lived more than 350 million years ago.

Option 2: Fossil Excavation Guide

Finding and excavating fossils requires patience. You have to know the best places to look, such as in sedimentary rock. Once you find a fossil, you want to excavate it very carefully. Fossils are delicate and break easily. Also, the position and location fossils are found in can tell scientists how the organism lived and died. Find out about fossil-excavation methods and make a guide for other students who want to find fossil treasures. Give some examples of information that paleontologists might learn from the excavation site.

Paleontologists in China carefully move dirt away from a skeleton.

Earth Science: Weather

Concept

Weather: Scientists record patterns of weather across different times and areas to make predictions about what kind of weather might happen next.

Lesson Objectives

- Students describe components of weather.
- Students identify weather patterns.
- Students discover tools that scientists use to measure and predict the weather.

Learning Approach

The learning path in this unit is designed to take students through different phases of learning based on the 5E model. This approach allows students to explore and connect to an idea through relatable activities, to build on prior knowledge and experience, to construct meaning, and to use or apply their understanding of a concept in a creative way.

Teacher Resource Page

Student Pages

Engage

Weather

Introduce the Concept

Distribute or display the unit concept page. Read the Spark Question and ask students to think about it. Have students identify the different weather events shown in the photos. Ask them what kinds of measurements could be made for each weather event shown. Next, use the text in the Discussion Guide (read it or paraphrase it) to facilitate a conversation that encourages students to share what they know about predicting and preparing for weather. Use Think-Pair-Share, a whole-class discussion, or any other format that suits your class.

Spark Question

How can we predict the weather?

Discussion Guide: Predicting the Future

What is weather? How would you describe the weather outside right now? What are some different kinds of weather? Is the weather the same every day? How often does it change? How much does it change? What tools can you think of that we use to measure weather changes? What are some clues that the weather might be changing? Why might it help us to know how it's changing? Have you ever been in extreme weather? Has school, or anything else, ever been closed or canceled because of the weather? Meteorologists are scientists who study weather. Sometimes weather can be predicted, but sometimes it can't. Meteorologists use lots of tools, from thermometers to satellites, to help them. In this unit, you will learn what causes different kinds of weather patterns and how scientists measure the causes.

Explore Activity Preparation

You may prefer to do the spraying for each pair of students, especially if your students do not have safety goggles. If any student is allergic to scents or sprays, have the student watch from several yards (meters) away. The student can return as soon as the cup is covered again. Plan how students will discard the water between trials (have a bucket or large bowl handy if your classroom does not have a sink).

Weather

Cloud Model

You will work in pairs to explore how clouds form.

What You'll Need

- safety goggles
- a clear cup
- hot water
- an ice pack or a small bowl of ice
- disinfectant spray or hairspray
- a pencil

What You'll Do

1. Put on your safety goggles.
2. **Trial 1:** Fill the cup ¼ full with hot water.
3. Cover the top of the cup completely with the ice pack or bowl of ice. Slowly count to 30.
4. One partner removes the ice pack or ice. The other partner quickly sprays one squirt into the cup. The first partner quickly replaces the ice pack or ice on top of the cup.
5. Count to 10 slowly and observe what happens inside the cup during that time. Remove the ice pack or ice and observe. Record your observations on the next page. Discard the water.
6. **Trial 2:** Repeat steps 2 through 4. This time, count to 90 before opening the cup. Observe what is on the inside of the cup near the top. Record your observations. Discard the water.
7. **Trial 3:** Repeat steps 2 and 3. This time, open the cup and close it without spraying. Record your observations. Discard the water.
8. Then answer the questions.

Explore

Weather

Observations

Name ______________________

1. Record your observations in the table.

Trial	Action	Observations
1	after spraying and counting to 10	
	after opening the cup	
2	after spraying and counting to 90	
	after opening the cup	
3	after counting to 30	

Preliminary Explanation

2. Why do you think the water needed to be hot?

____

3. Why do you think the cup needed to be covered with something cold?

____

4. What could the spray be modeling in real weather?

____

Weather

Measure Weather Today to Predict for Tomorrow

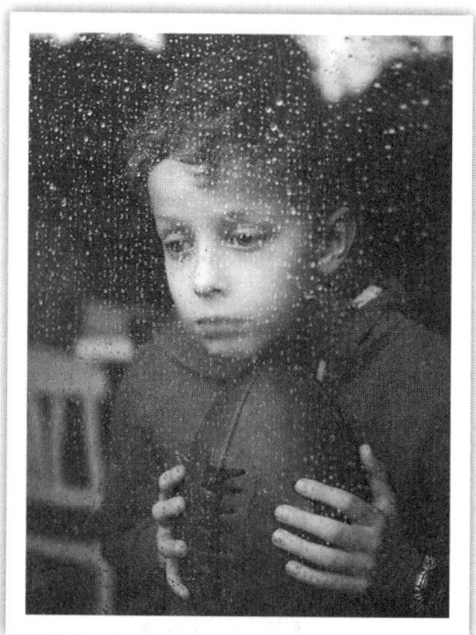

Your family planned a big family picnic at the park. You and your cousins will play outside, and everyone will eat pizza and cake at the picnic tables. Then, on the day of your picnic, surprise! It's pouring rain and everyone has to move inside. Oh no! If you'd known that was going to happen, you could've planned different activities or held the picnic on a different day. People often want to know what the weather will be like. Let's take a look at weather and how **meteorologists** predict it.

Earth's Atmosphere, Where Weather Forms

Layers of gases circle Earth and stretch for hundreds of miles (kilometers) above it. These layers are the **atmosphere**. The air we breathe is part of the atmosphere. **Weather** is what is happening in the atmosphere in a certain place and time. Weather changes as the atmosphere changes. The atmosphere soaks up heat from the sun's rays. It also sends some of the heat back into space. This is how the atmosphere keeps Earth's temperatures from becoming too hot or too cold.

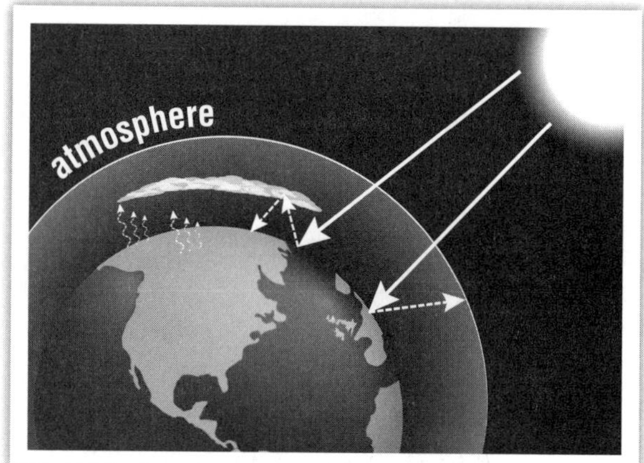

The atmosphere surrounds Earth and keeps it warm.

The atmosphere has weight. It presses down on Earth and everything on it. It presses down harder in some places than in other places. The amount it presses is called air pressure. Meteorologists measure and study air pressure. They have noticed air pressure patterns. Colder air tends to have higher pressure than normal. It is heavier and sinks toward the ground. It dries the air, so it usually brings good weather. Air with lower pressure than normal is warmer. It usually moves upward and causes high winds, clouds, and rain.

Clouds and Rain

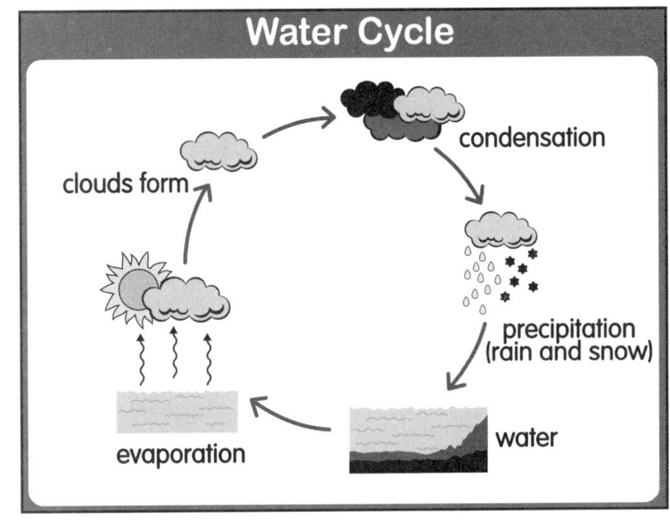

The atmosphere holds water in the form of **vapor**. Water vapor is made when water changes from a liquid to a gas by **evaporation**. The vapor seems to disappear into the air, but it's still there. If water vapor is lifted high enough into the air, it cools. Cooling causes the vapor to form **condensation**. These tiny drops collect and form clouds. When the droplets become heavy enough, they fall to the ground as **precipitation**. Rain, snow, sleet, and hail are all types of precipitation. When the temperature warms up, much of that precipitation evaporates back into vapor again. This cycle of water going into the air and coming back down is known as the **water cycle**.

There are different types of clouds. Scientists group clouds into three main types. You can tell each type of cloud by its shape and by how high it is in the sky. There is a pattern to each type of cloud and the weather it brings.

Cirrus (SEAR-uhs) clouds are thin and feathery. They are found highest in the sky. Cirrus clouds are a sign that the weather may change.

Cumulus (KYOO-myuh-luhs) clouds are puffy white clouds, lower than cirrus clouds. They bring mostly fair weather, but sometimes they bring thunderstorms and hail.

Stratus (STRAY-tuhs) clouds are the lowest clouds. They look like a flat gray sheet. Light rain or snow may fall from stratus clouds. Fog is stratus clouds that are close to the ground.

Explain Weather

Tools to Measure Weather

We can't change the weather, but we can measure it. Both the sun and your food may be hot, but they don't feel the same. A **thermometer** is used to measure temperature so we know just how hot something is. A thermometer gives us a number on a scale, such as 98° Fahrenheit (37° Celsius). We can also measure the amount of rain. Instead of saying "It rained cats and dogs today!" a **rain gauge** tells us exactly how much rain fell.

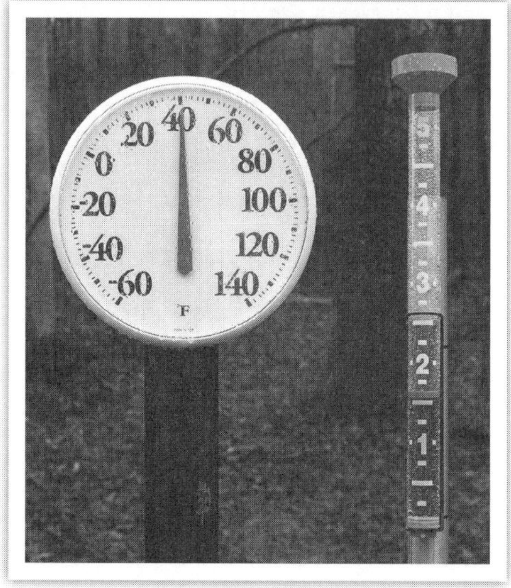

Changes in the weather happen when the wind changes speed and direction. That's why meteorologists use special tools to measure wind speed and direction. An **anemometer** (ann-ih-MOM-uh-tur) is a tool that measures how fast the wind is blowing. The faster the anemometer spins, the faster the wind is blowing. A **wind vane** points in the direction the wind is blowing from. These tools tell us how strong a storm is and the direction the storm is moving.

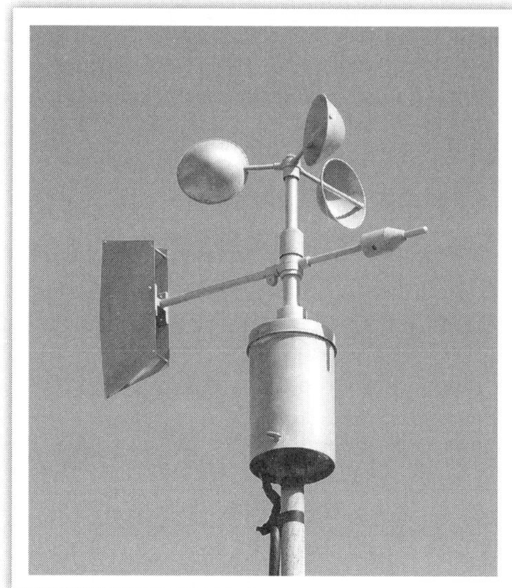

Predicting Weather

Meteorologists use all of these tools, and more, to form a "picture" of what our weather will be. For example, let's say that satellite photos show a storm over the ocean. The wind speed and direction tell us that the storm will travel toward land where people are. Meteorologists can warn people in that area. Measuring changes in air pressure and observing cloud types are some other ways scientists use patterns to predict weather. When people know what the weather will look like, they can prepare and plan for it.

Weather

Concept Vocabulary

anemometer:
a tool that measures wind speed

atmosphere:
the layers of gases that circle Earth

condensation:
the changing of a gas into a liquid

evaporation:
the changing of a liquid into a gas

meteorologist:
a scientist who studies weather

precipitation:
water that falls as rain, snow, sleet, or hail

rain gauge:
a tool that measures rainfall

thermometer:
a tool that measures temperature

vapor:
the gas that clouds are made of

water cycle:
the way water moves in different forms through the atmosphere

weather:
what happens in the atmosphere; what the air is like outside

wind vane:
a tool that shows wind direction

Notes

Evaluate

Weather

Vocabulary Review

Name ______________________________

Complete the sentences using concept vocabulary terms.

1. When a cloud collects enough water ___ ___ ___ ___ [ ], it rains.
2. Most people like sunny ___ [ ] ___ ___ ___ ___ ___, but I like it foggy.
3. My aunt used a ___ ___ ___ ___ ___ ___ ___ ___ ___ ___ ___ to check my cousin's temperature when he was sick.
4. The [ ] ___ ___ ___ ___ ___ ___ ___ ___ ___ protects our planet in many ways.
5. Jamila read the ___ ___ ___ ___   ___ ___ [ ] ___ ___ after last night's storm.
6. I refill my dog's water bowl daily because of ___ ___ ___ ___ ___ ___ ___ ___ ___ ___ [ ].
7. I wonder how many times a drop of water goes through the ___ ___ ___ ___ ___   ___ ___ ___ [ ] ___ in a year.
8. My coat keeps me dry in all kinds of ___ ___ ___ ___ ___ ___ ___ ___ [ ] ___ ___ ___ ___.
9. The way the ___ ___ ___ [ ] ___ ___ ___ ___ ___ ___ is spinning around, I should go fly a kite!
10. Milo wiped the ___ ___ ___ ___ ___ ___ ___ ___ ___ ___ ___ ___ off the outside of the cold soda can.
11. The ___ ___ ___ ___ ___ ___ ___ [ ] ___ ___ ___ ___ ___ checks weather instruments several times a day.
12. The ___ ___ ___ ___   ___ ___ ___ ___ usually points to the east in the morning.

Now arrange all of the letters in boxes above to answer the riddle.

What goes up when rain comes down?

___ ___   ___ ___ b ___ ___ ___ ___ ___

Evaluate

Weather

Concept Comprehension

Name ______________________

1. True or false: Weather happens in the atmosphere. ______________

2. How does water get into the atmosphere?

____

How do clouds and rain form?

____

____

3. Some students asked questions about the weather. Choose the best tool to answer each question.

thermometer	anemometer	wind vane	rain gauge

a. Which way is the wind blowing? ______________

b. How hot is it outside? ______________

c. How fast is the wind blowing? ______________

d. How much rain fell yesterday? ______________

4. Circle the underlined part that answers the question.

a. Does temperature tell how warm **or** how wet something is?

b. Is snow atmosphere **or** precipitation?

c. Does an anemometer measure wind speed **or** direction?

d. Does a meteorologist predict the weather **or** study space?

e. Is water vapor in the ocean **or** in the atmosphere?

Weather

5. Label the diagram of the water cycle. Use the words below.

land	sun	clouds	ocean	precipitation	evaporation

6. What is the sun's role in the water cycle?

____

7. What do you think happens to clouds after it rains?

____

8. Where does condensation take place?

____

Where the air pressure is higher than normal, the weather is usually good. Where the air pressure is lower than normal, the weather often brings storms. Use this information and the map to answer questions 9 through 11.

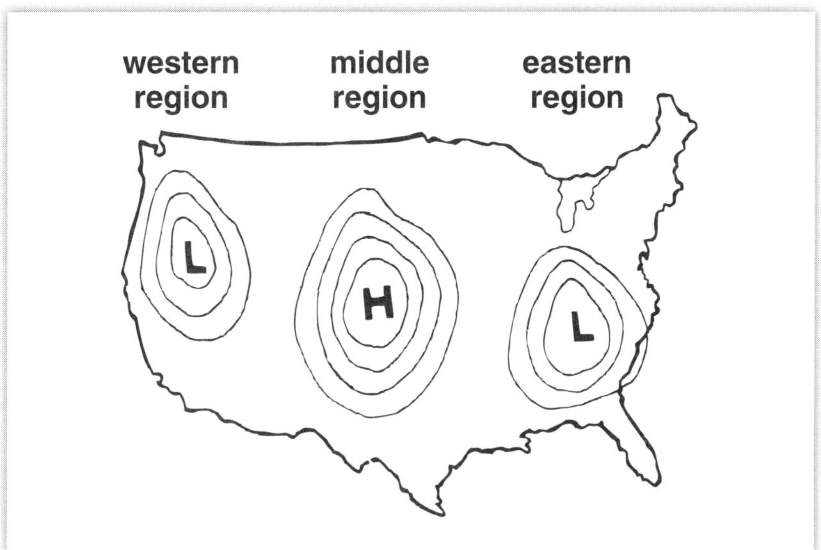

9. How many pressure regions does the map show? ______________________

10. Which region probably has good weather? ______________________

11. It's raining today. Your local meteorologist says that high air pressure is moving into your area tomorrow. What do you predict the weather will be like tomorrow?

____

12. Windmills are used to produce clean energy. The more a windmill's blades spin, the more energy it produces. A power company is going to set up some new windmills. What information should the company collect to decide where to place the windmills?

____

____

____

Weather

Reflect

Name ______________________

What is your favorite type of weather? Describe what it's like outside during that weather. In what season or seasons does this weather usually happen? What do you like to do during your favorite weather?

Weather

Imagine

Name________________________

Imagine that you are a raindrop that falls to the ground. You make a splash landing in a puddle on the playground. Tell a story about how you got there. Describe your trip through the water cycle.

Extend

Weather

Project

Choose one of the project options below.

Option 1: Weather Report

Practice being a weather reporter! Watch some TV or online weather reports to get an idea of the kind of information that is reported. Then print out a map of a country and fill in the weather that happened at various times on that day. You can include fog, rain, snow, temperatures, how windy it was, or any other weather event. Record yourself describing the day's weather across different parts of the country, especially any extreme weather. Bonus: Try making a weather prediction for the following day!

Option 2: Weather Safety Poster

Weather is different in different places. What kind of weather happens in your area? Some examples might include thunderstorms, blizzards, tornadoes, flash floods, or hurricanes. Find out what you can do to prepare. Ask what preparations have been done at home and at school. Create a poster showing what people should do to prepare and stay safe.

Earth Science: Climate

Concept

Climate: Climate describes a range of an area's typical weather conditions and how those conditions vary over years.

Lesson Objectives

- Students differentiate between weather and climate.
- Students analyze and interpret data to determine a region's climate zone.

Learning Approach

The learning path in this unit is designed to take students through different phases of learning based on the 5E model. This approach allows students to explore and connect to an idea through relatable activities, to build on prior knowledge and experience, to construct meaning, and to use or apply their understanding of a concept in a creative way.

Teacher Resource Page

Student Pages

Engage

Climate

Introduce the Concept

Distribute or display the unit concept page. Read the Spark Question and ask students to think about it. Have students study the photos. Then ask students to guess the place, or type of ecosystem, where each photo was taken. Encourage students to look for clues, such as the animal and plants that are shown or the clothing the people are wearing. Ask what they think each place is like at different times of year. Next, use the text in the Discussion Guide (read it or paraphrase it) to facilitate a conversation that encourages students to think about what it is like outside throughout the year where they live. Use Think-Pair-Share, a whole-class discussion, or any other format that suits your class.

Spark Question

Why is it sometimes cold in a warm climate?

Discussion Guide: Weather vs. Climate

Look outside the window. What is the weather like today? Has it been like this all season? What will the weather will be like here in the other seasons? How do you know? Do you have a relative or friend who lives far away where the seasons are different? How are they different? These places have different climates. A climate is a pattern of weather that repeats year after year. For example, the pattern in most deserts is hot and dry weather most of the year, but it rains occasionally in winter, and the temperature does cool off. In this unit, you will learn about different climates around the world and the reasons they are different.

Explore Activity Preparation

If your students have access to the Internet, provide them with a link to a website that shows average or usual temperatures for your region. National government weather websites, such as NOAA in the United States, are usually good sources. If technology is not an option in your classroom, provide information in print form. If needed, explain that precipitation is the amount of rain, snow, hail, and sleet that falls in a specific place.

Climate

David Talukdar / Shutterstock.com

Explore

Climate

Climate Investigation

You will work in pairs to figure out what the climate is like where you live.

What You'll Need

- weather data
- a pencil

What You'll Do

1. You and your partner will research the usual temperatures for each month of the year in the area where you live. Record your data in the data table on the next page.
2. Next, research the usual rainfall and snowfall amounts for each month in your area. Record your data.
3. Then answer the questions. Use the table below to answer question 6.

Five Major Climate Zones

Tropical	Dry	Continental	Temperate	Polar
This zone receives a lot of sunlight and rain. It is usually very warm in this climate.	This zone is very hot during the day and it can be very cold at night. This zone receives a lot of sun but not a lot of rain or clouds.	This zone has cold, snowy winters and hot summers. There are large differences in temperature between the seasons.	This zone has cool or cold winters and warm or hot summers. The weather in the spring and fall is not too hot and not too cold.	This zone is always very cold and dry. It doesn't receive much rain or snow. But there is always snow on the ground because it doesn't melt.

Explore

Climate

Data

Name ____________________

1. Record the usual temperatures, rainfall, and snowfall in your area.

Usual Monthly Weather for ____________________

	Jan	Feb	Mar	Apr	May	Jun	Jul	Aug	Sep	Oct	Nov	Dec
Usual daytime temperature												
Usual nighttime temperature												
Usual amount of rainfall												
Usual amount of snowfall												

Analysis

Use the table above to answer questions 2 through 5.

2. Look at the daytime temperatures for every month. How much do they change? What is the temperature mostly like during the day? When is it usually hot, warm, cold, or cool? What patterns do you see?

____

____

____

Climate

3. Look at the nighttime temperatures for every month. Compare them to the daytime temperatures. Do they change as much or more? What patterns do you see?

____

____

____

4. Look at the rainfall amounts for every month. What patterns do you see? Does it rain more or less during the winter and summer months? What are the temperatures like in the months with the most rain?

____

____

____

5. Look at the snowfall amounts for every month. What patterns do you see? What do you notice about the temperature and rainfall when it snows the most?

____

____

____

Preliminary Conclusion

6. Look at the climate zone table on page 128. Which climate zone do you think you live in? Why?

   I think I live in the ____________ zone because ____________

   ____

   ____

   ____.

Climate Around the Globe

Julio woke up one morning to a strange sound he had never heard before. Something was tapping on the roof of his mud house. He looked out the window and saw small falling drops. He ran outside and the drops wet his skin. It was the first time in his nine years of life that he had ever seen rain! Julio lives in the Atacama Desert in Chile. It has the driest **climate** on Earth. But for a short time that day, the weather was rainy.

What Is Climate?

Climate is the pattern of weather in a specific area over a long period of time, at least 30 years. Weather is what is happening in the air surrounding Earth right now in a specific place. The weather of a place can change hour by hour or day by day. It could be clear and sunny at the moment in Tokyo, Japan. But if the weather there is hardly ever clear and sunny, then Tokyo's climate is not clear and sunny. Unlike weather, changes in climate happen slowly, often over hundreds, thousands, or millions of years.

Climatologists are scientists who study climate. They look at temperature, **precipitation**, and wind data of a specific place over many years. Climatologists use weather tools, just as meteorologists do. But climatologists are measuring the effects of local weather. For example, they might take soil and water samples. Then they share and compare their data to look for patterns. They want to see if weather in a specific place changes, how often it changes, and how much it changes, from month to month and year to year. Studying these patterns gives them a "picture" of the climate. It's like taking your photo at school each year. You might cut your hair, wear different clothes, or grow a little, but the photo will give you a general idea of how you looked that year.

Explain Climate

The Sun's Role

No matter where you live, you see the sun up in the sky. It rises in the east and sets in the west. But how it moves from one side to the other is different. People who live near the **equator** see the sun for about 12 hours every single day. The sun travels highest in the sky throughout the year. People who live in the far north or far south see the sun much lower in the sky. Most of us live somewhere in between the equator and the poles. We see the sun somewhere in between.

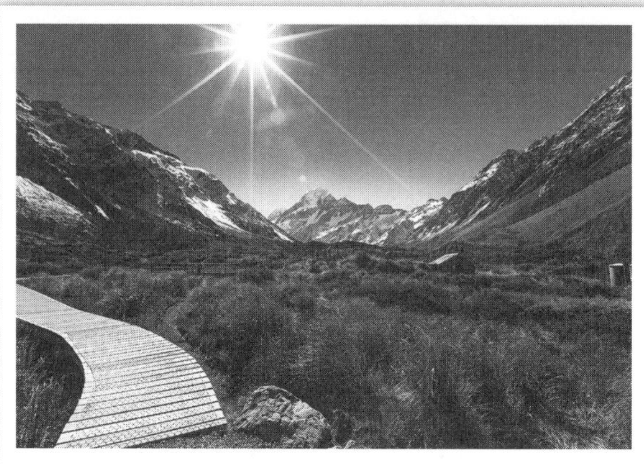

Noon in New Zealand, near the south end of the planet

The closer you live to the equator, the more directly the sun shines on you and the warmer your climate is. Imagine a heater blowing warm air. If you stand in front of it, you will warm up quickly. If you stand next to it, you will not get as warm because the heat is hitting only your side.

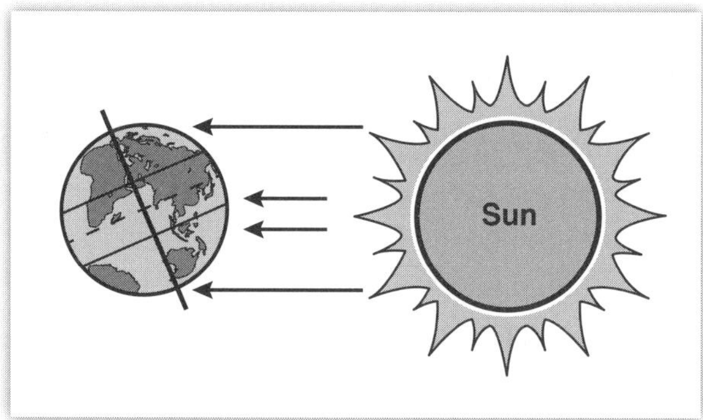

Places near the poles receive weaker energy from the sun.

elevation:
4,268 feet (1,300 meters)

Chilkat Range, Alaska

Climate Factors

The distance from the equator is one of four main **factors** that affect an area's climate. The distance from oceans or large lakes is another factor. Water makes the air moist, which makes winters and summers more mild. The third factor is an area's **elevation**, or its distance above the sea. High elevations, such as hills and mountains, tend to be colder. The amount of wind a place receives is the fourth factor. Wind moves cool air, heat, and moisture around.

Climate Zones

There are many different climates on Earth, but there are five main climate **zones**. These zones are tropical, dry, temperate, continental, and polar.

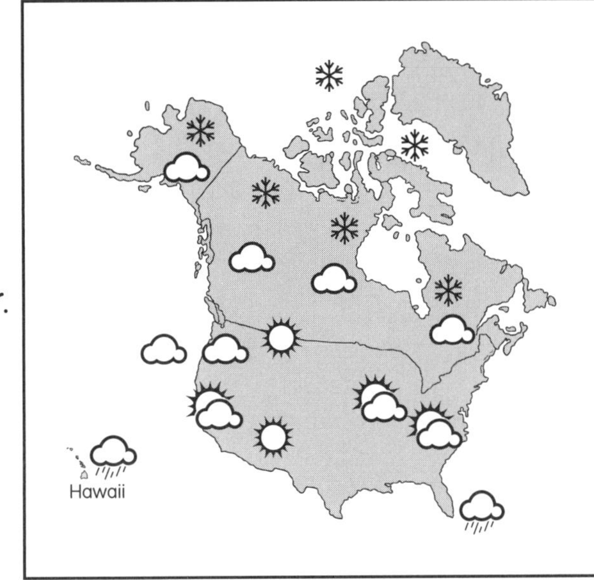

Legend

- dry
- polar
- tropical
- temperate
- continental

North America has land in all five main climate zones.

The tropical climate zone is found near the equator. Places in this zone receive lots of sunlight and rainfall and are usually warm. Many rainforests live in this climate.

Places in the dry climate zone do not receive a lot of rain. Temperatures during the day are usually very hot, while temperatures at night can be quite cold. Places with a dry climate usually receive a lot of sunlight. Deserts have dry climates.

If you live in the temperate zone, your winters are cool or cold and summers are warm or hot. The weather patterns for this climate depend on how close the place is to the ocean. The countries of Germany and New Zealand have this climate.

Places with a continental climate are always found above the equator. The continental climate is similar to the temperate climate, but the differences between summer and winter are greater.

The polar climate zone is the coldest on Earth. These places receive less direct sunlight. Temperatures are extremely low during the winter, and precipitation is very rare. However, they receive some precipitation in the form of snow. Antarctica is a continent with a polar climate.

Our one Earth has many different faces!

Explain

Climate

Concept Vocabulary

climate:
the pattern of weather in an area over a long period of time

climatologist:
a scientist who studies climate

elevation:
the height of a place above the sea

equator:
an imaginary line around the middle of Earth that divides the planet in half

factor:
something that affects what happens

precipitation:
water falling from the clouds as rain, snow, hail, or sleet

zone:
an area that has a special characteristic or purpose

Notes

Climate

Vocabulary Review

Name ____________________

Read each sentence that uses a concept vocabulary term.
Then write your own sentence using the term.

1. Changes in **climate** happen very slowly.

   ____

2. The **climatologist** checked the soil after a year with no rain.

   ____

3. The Chilkat mountain range has an **elevation** of 1,300 meters.

   ____

4. The sun shines more directly near the **equator**.

   ____

5. There are four main **factors** that affect climate.

   ____

6. The scientist examined the **precipitation** data.

   ____

7. The climate is different in each **zone**.

   ____

Climate

Concept Comprehension

Name ______________________________

1. Look at the world map. Notice where each type of climate is found. Write three patterns of climate that you can see.

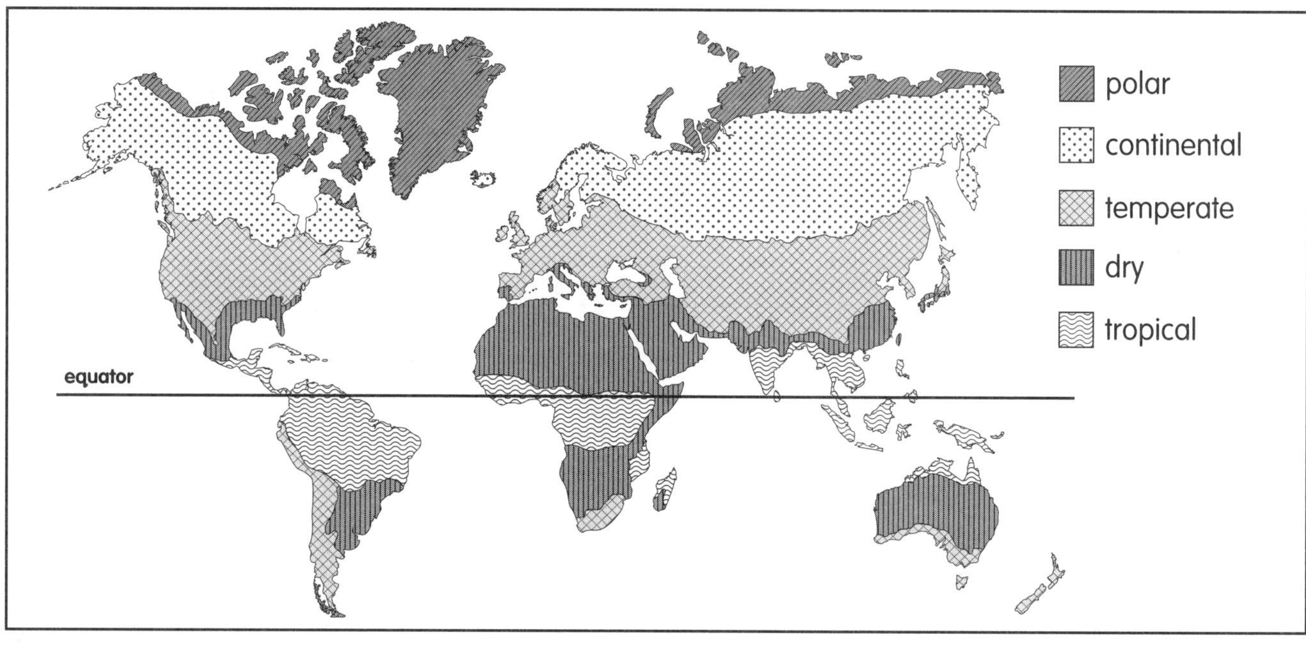

____

____

____

____

2. Look at the picture. Which town do you think has a cooler climate? Explain why.

____

____

____

____

____

3. Why do regions near the equator have warmer climates than other regions around the world?

____

____

4. List four factors that affect the climate of a place.

____

____

____

____

5. Look at the map of two cities in the United States. San Diego, California, and Phoenix, Arizona, are the same distance north from the equator. However, they have different climates. San Diego has warm summers and cool winters. Phoenix has very hot summers and mild winters. Give one reason why these two cities have different climates.

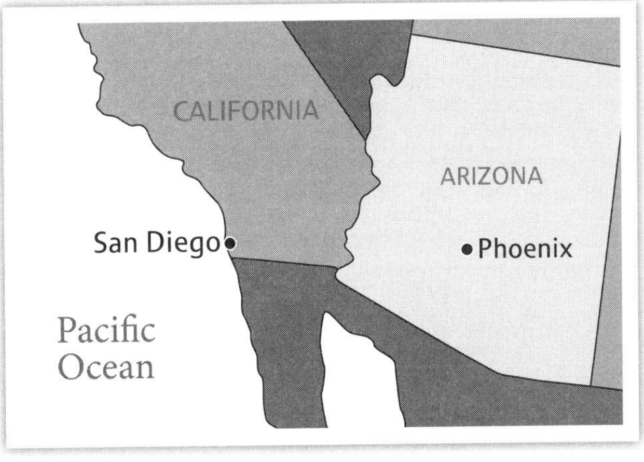

____

____

____

6. Complete the sentence with the words **weather** and **climate**.

________________ is what you expect, but ________________ is what you get.

Extend

Climate

Justify

Name ____________________

When you grow up, you can choose to live in any climate you want. Think about the different climate zones. Which one would you most like to live in? Explain why and describe what it would be like to live there. State what you could do there that you couldn't do in other climate zones.

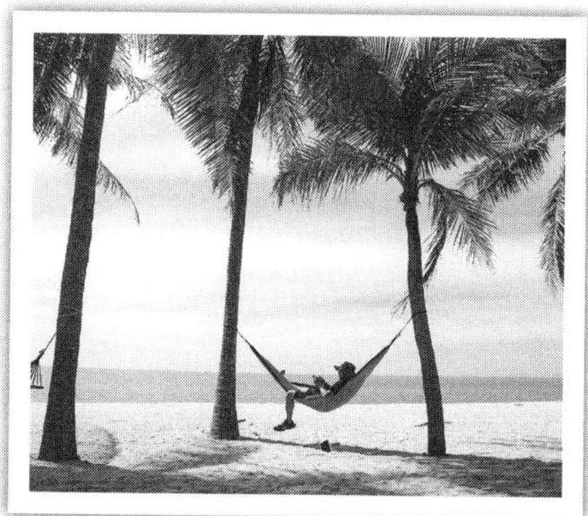

Climate

Apply

Name ______________________________

It is very important for farmers to pay attention to their climate zone. Different fruit and vegetable plants grow in different conditions. Some need to go through a freeze every year, yet others will die if they freeze. Some like lots of rain, and others will rot in too much rain. Even farmers who raise animals for meat are affected by climate zones, because some animals eat grass or other live plants.

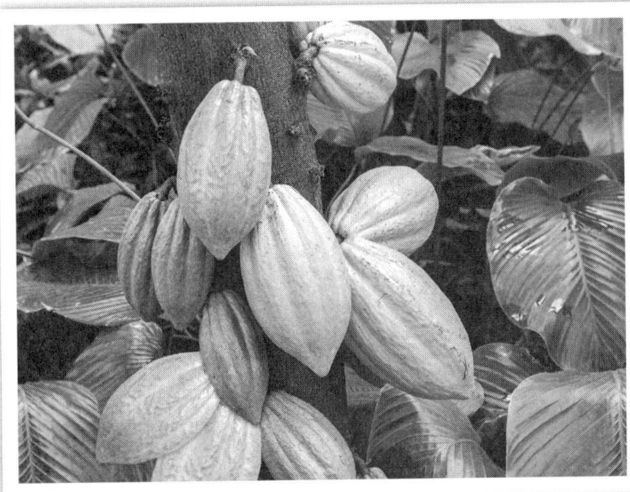

Cacao trees grow giant pods full of cocoa beans. The beans are used to make chocolate. These trees grow under other trees in tropical rainforests.

Imagine that you are a farmer. Decide what crop you want to grow or what animal you want to raise. You can choose something that grows where you live, or you can decide to live somewhere else. Then describe the needs of your crop or animal. State which climate zone you are farming in. Explain why that zone is a good place for your farm.

____

____

____

____

____

____

____

____

____

Extend Climate

Project

Choose one of the project options below.

Option 1: Climate Change Display

Make a poster or slideshow to teach others about climate change. Include a short explanation of what climate change is. Explain how it affects all living things. Describe its causes. Provide some data about climate change. Include things people can do to slow climate change.

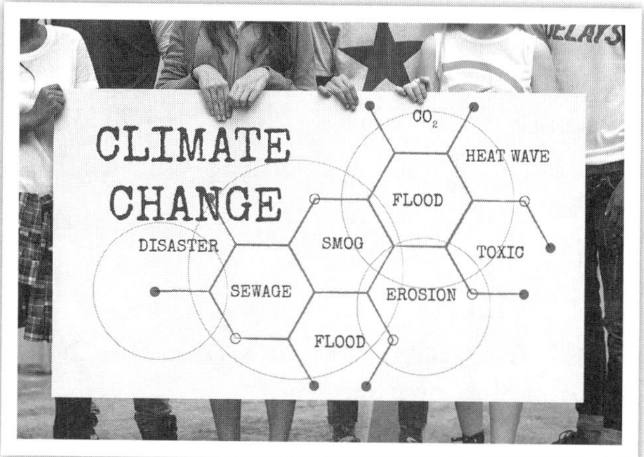

Option 2: House for the Climate

Design and build a model of a house for a tropical, polar, or desert climate. Think about the different weather in the climate zone you choose. Will it have to protect the people who live there from rain, heat, cold, wind, or snow?

Use natural and machine-made materials that you find around your house. Some natural materials are grass, leaves, twigs, and dirt or mud. Machine-made materials can include aluminum foil, cardboard, cotton balls, craft sticks, paper clips, paper roll tubes, modeling clay, plastic wrap, and straws.

The shape of the roof on this cabin helps snow slide off.

Earth Science:
Natural Processes and Hazards

Concept

Natural Hazards: A variety of hazards result from natural processes. Humans can take steps to reduce their impacts.

Lesson Objectives

- Students discover types of natural disasters and how they form.
- Students describe ways that people protect themselves from natural disasters.

Learning Approach

The learning path in this unit is designed to take students through different phases of learning based on the 5E model. This approach allows students to explore and connect to an idea through relatable activities, to build on prior knowledge and experience, to construct meaning, and to use or apply their understanding of a concept in a creative way.

Teacher Resource Page

Student Pages

Engage

Natural Processes and Hazards

Introduce the Concept

Distribute or display the unit concept page. Have students study the natural hazards and their effects in the photos. Read the Spark Question and ask students to think about it. Next, use the text in the Discussion Guide (read it or paraphrase it) to facilitate a conversation that encourages students to share what they know about natural hazards and how to prepare for them. Use Think-Pair-Share, a whole-class discussion, or any other format that suits your class.

Spark Question

How can we stay safe in a flood?

Discussion Guide: Protecting Ourselves

What kinds of natural hazards do you see in the photos? Some of these tend to happen in certain parts of the world, and some can happen anywhere. What are some causes of natural hazards? Have you ever been in a scary situation caused by a natural hazard? What types of natural hazards are possible in your neighborhood? What plans do you have at home to protect yourself and your family? What do we do here at school to prepare? In this unit, you will learn about the natural processes that cause some hazards and how to stay safe.

Note to teacher: Natural hazards can be a scary topic. Adjust the discussion and any activity as needed to be sensitive to any past traumas. Discuss with your students steps they can take to protect themselves and their loved ones. Doing so reinforces a sense that we do have some control over our safety, a key point in this unit. If possible, bring in a speaker such as a firefighter, a paramedic, or someone from the Red Cross to discuss disaster preparedness.

Explore Activity Preparation

Gather the materials in a central location in the classroom for groups to access as needed. For testing their model houses, have a plastic bin or sink, bigger than a shoebox, with 1 inch (2.5 centimeters) of water in it.

Engage

Natural Processes and Hazards

Volcano eruption

Lava flow

Flooded river

Crack in the ground from an earthquake

Tornado

Forest fire

Flood-Safe House Model

You will work in groups of four to design and build a model house that will not be affected by a flood.

What You'll Need

- modeling clay
- plastic wrap
- aluminum foil
- plastic water bottles
- plastic food containers
- cardboard
- clean frozen-food trays
- straws
- craft sticks
- plastic toy bricks
- foam bricks
- aluminum cans
- string or zip ties
- paper and pencil
- scissors
- a shoebox
- a spray bottle of water

What You'll Do

1. Brainstorm ideas for your house. It must be no larger than a shoebox. It must be able to sit in 1 inch (2.5 centimeters) of water without being damaged. Think about how different materials act when they get wet. Think about how to keep rain and floodwater out of the house. Think about its roof and the structure below its floor. Sketch your ideas on paper.
2. Start building your house. Use the materials that you think will work best. You can make changes to your plan as you go if something isn't working. Listen to and try out everyone's ideas. Take notes about which materials are working and which ones aren't.
3. When your house has been built, you will test it by setting it in water and spraying water on top of it.
4. Then complete the questions on the next page.

Explore

Natural Processes and Hazards

Observations

Name ______________________

1. Which materials worked the best? Why?

2. Which materials didn't work well? Why?

Preliminary Conclusion

3. Now that you have tested your group's house model and you have seen the other house models from your classmates, describe how a house should be built to survive a flood.

4. What other factors might help protect people and homes from a flood?

5. Why is it important to think about possible hazards when building a home?

Natural Processes and Hazards

Sometimes Nature Plays Rough

Nature gives us many beautiful things to enjoy and resources to use. But sometimes nature gives us challenges. Scientists who study natural hazards are getting better at understanding them. Scientists are learning what causes these challenges and how they affect our planet and our lives. Someday they may be able to control these challenges. For now, let's look at what some of them do and what we can do about them.

Earthquakes

Earth is made up of layers. All the land and the oceans, along with the people, are on the surface. The surface and the part just below it are the **crust**. The crust is broken into pieces like a broken dinner plate. But they are much larger. Some are as large as an ocean or a continent. Just below those broken pieces is very thick melted rock. It's in a layer called the **mantle**.

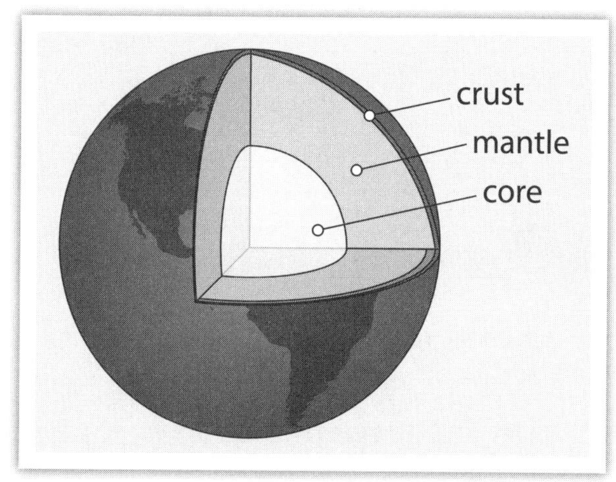

Think about the ice floating in this photo. Sometimes the ice pieces bump directly into each other. Other times they slide past each other. If there were ants sitting on top of those pieces of ice, what would they feel? You guessed it: earthquakes!

Earthquakes happen when the broken pieces of Earth's crust suddenly move. Sometimes the pieces separate. Other times, they bump together or their rough edges scrape past each other, which causes shaking.

Scientists have tools that tell them an earthquake is starting. But they find out only a few seconds before we can feel it. Some pets also feel the shaking just before people do and try to hide from it. When the shaking first starts, people should move somewhere safe. They should get away from anything that might fall. They can crawl under something strong, such as a table, until the shaking stops. People who live where earthquakes are common can store earthquake supplies, such as flashlights, food, bottled water, and first-aid kits.

Volcanoes

Sometimes **magma**, the melted rock from the mantle, reaches Earth's surface through a **volcano**. About 1,500 volcanoes on Earth are active. This means that they have erupted recently and could erupt again in the future.

We see volcanoes rise high above Earth's surface, but they start below it. Volcanoes form when hot, soft rock rises up from the mantle through cracks in the crust. The hot rock is always moving, like boiling water in a pot. As the rock gets closer to the crust, gases push against it. When a volcano erupts, magma pushes up through the center of the volcano and out of its **vent** on top. When magma reaches the surface, it is called **lava**. As lava cools, it turns from a liquid into a solid. Now it is hard rock.

Inside a Volcano

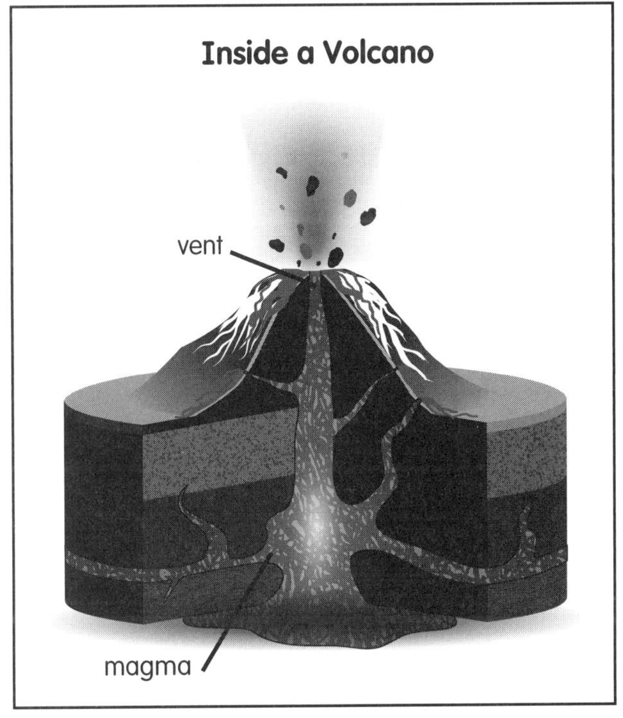

Volcanoes give clues when they are getting close to erupting. The temperature in the volcano goes up, and gases start to come out of the vent. There may also be an increase in earthquakes nearby. If it looks like a volcano is about to erupt, officials will tell people to leave the area.

Natural Processes and Hazards

Floods

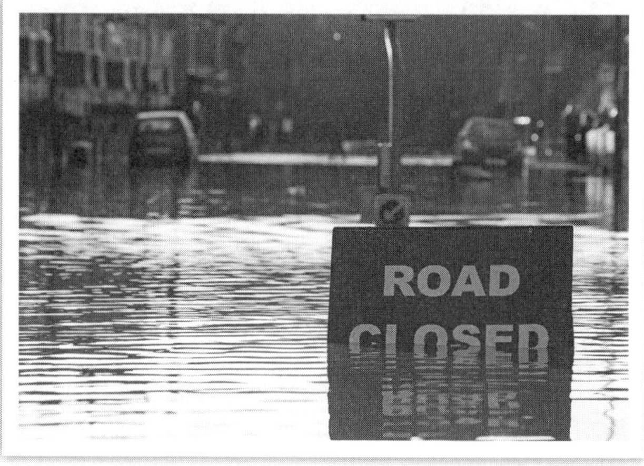

A **flood** is a body of water covering an area of land that is usually dry. Areas near rivers, lakes, and oceans can flood. River floods are the most common. Many rivers have a cycle of dry times and flooding. Rivers and lakes may flow over their **banks** when there is more rain than usual or when snow and ice melt quickly. Hurricanes can cause floods along coasts. Rainstorms can cause floods anywhere. Floods are sometimes helpful. They can bring new soil to an area. But floods can cause a lot of damage. Farms and crops may be destroyed. Floods can trap people in cars and homes. More lives are lost in floods than in any other kind of weather. Floods destroy property. Rebuilding a city again after a flood can cost billions of dollars.

Meteorologists know when flooding is possible, and they warn the public several days in advance. It's a good time to leave the area until the water can soak into the ground, flow away, or evaporate. If you are ever caught in a flood, move up to higher ground or even to a higher floor. Do not try to walk, swim, or ride in a vehicle through a flooded area. Leave if you are told to do so.

Sometimes, flooding is controlled with a **dam**. Dams are built to collect water for use later on. They have gates that open to let water out when needed, such as for farms. The energy from falling water can be turned into electricity.

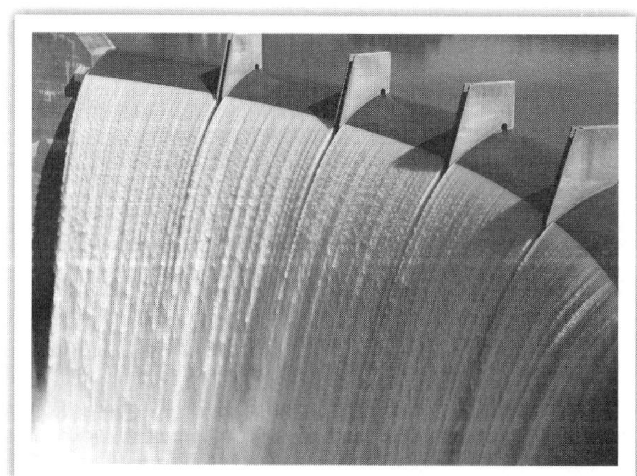

Englebright Dam on the Yuba River in California

No matter where you live, natural processes happen all around us. By learning about them, we can stay safe wherever we live.

Explain

Natural Processes and Hazards

Concept Vocabulary

bank:
the land at the edge of a river

crust:
the top layer of Earth

dam:
a structure that holds back water

earthquake:
an event in which the ground in an area shakes

flood:
water covering land that is usually dry

lava:
molten rock that has erupted from a volcano

magma:
thick melted rock in the mantle of Earth

mantle:
the layer below Earth's crust

vent:
an opening that lets out gases and liquids

volcano:
an opening in Earth's crust that releases lava, ash, and steam

Notes

Natural Processes and Hazards

Vocabulary Review

Name ______________________________

Complete the paragraphs using concept vocabulary terms.

1. The Nile River in Africa is the longest river in the world. In ancient times in Egypt, water flowed over the ______________ of the Nile River every year, causing a ______________. Today, there is a huge ______________ on the Nile at Aswan, Egypt. It was built in 1970. It controls extra water in the rainy season and stores it to be used later.

2. The country of Chile is located on the coast of the Pacific Ocean. There is a crack underneath the sea where two pieces of Earth's ______________ meet. In 2010, there was a strong ______________ in Chile. Buildings were destroyed. The shaking caused giant waves in the ocean, which came onshore. The homes of many people were washed away.

Natural Processes and Hazards

3. Nearly 150 years ago in 1883, the Krakatoa _______________ erupted in the country of Indonesia. Enormous amounts of _______________ rose from the _______________. Some of the _______________ that came out of Krakatoa's _______________ flowed into the sea and boiled the water into steam. The eruption was so huge that it destroyed most of the island it was on. The sound could be heard in Australia, more than 2,000 miles (3,600 kilometers) away!

Evaluate

Natural Processes and Hazards

Concept Comprehension

Name 

1. Label the parts of the volcano using the words **crust**, **lava**, and **magma**.

   a. ____________________

   b. ____________________

   c. ____________________

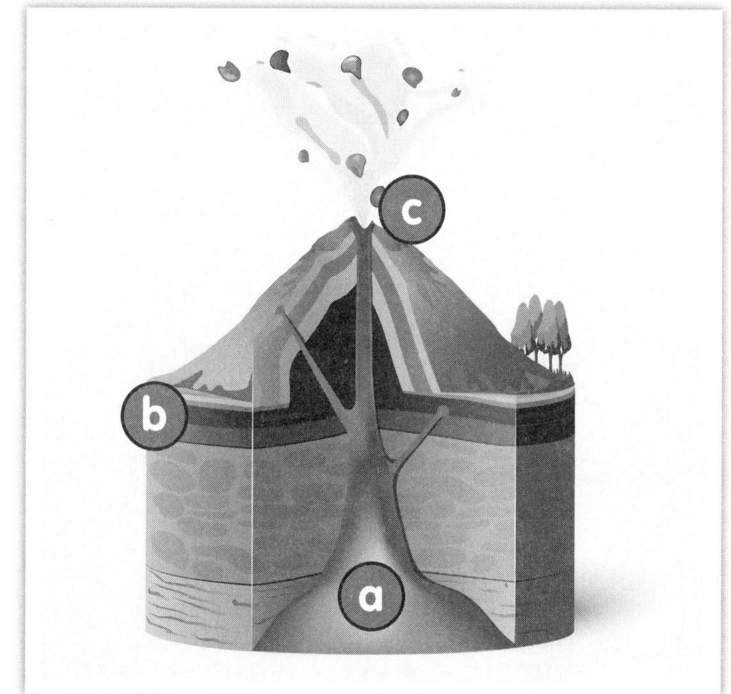

2. Where does magma comes from?

   a. the sky

   b. the crust

   c. the ocean

   d. the mantle

3. What causes earthquakes?

   a. crust breaking into small pieces

   b. ice sliding on top of the crust

   c. pieces of crust hitting or scraping each other

   d. pieces of crust coming up from the mantle

4. Which of these is true about floods?

   a. Floods are hard to predict.

   b. Floods have several causes.

   c. Floods happen mostly on the coasts.

   d. Floods are not as dangerous as other hazards.

5. People should be prepared before a natural disaster happens because they may not have electricity and may not be able to buy food or water. What other things would you need to have? Why would you need them?

____

____

____

____

6. Write one way that floods are helpful and one way they are harmful.

   Helpful: _______________

   Harmful: _______________

7. How do dams help control flooding?

____

____

8. Write three ways to stay safe in a flood.

____

____

____

9. Why do you think scientists are trying to find ways to predict natural hazards?

____

____

____

Natural Processes and Hazards

Reflect

Name ____________________

Imagine that there was a natural disaster and you had to leave your home. Write what items you would take with you and explain why. You can take only what you can carry.

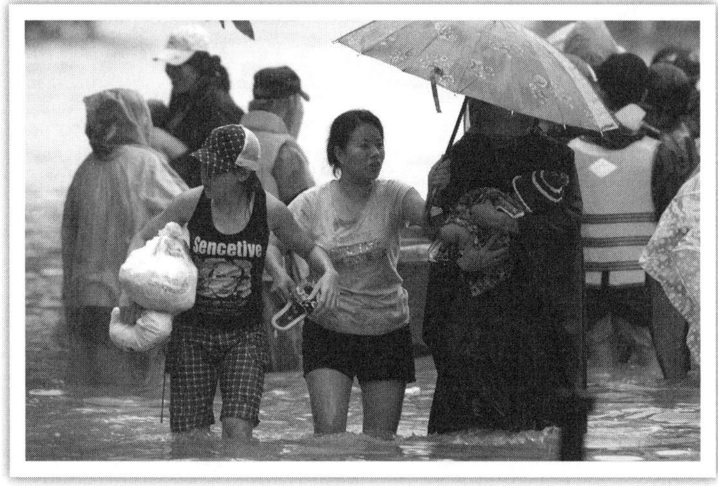

Marc van Vuren / Shutterstock.com

Natural Processes and Hazards

Compose

Name ______________________

Science poems can be a fun way to learn and remember science concepts. Write a poem about volcanoes. Use some of the vocabulary words from this unit. Hint: For rhyming poems, end sentences with words that are easy to rhyme.

It can flow and it can run.
It disappears out in the sun.
It can trickle and can freeze.
It takes a lot to fill the seas.
We use it for drinking
and washing and growing.
I'm sure that by now
you surely are knowing
The name of this wet
and wonderful stuff.
It's WATER, of course,
There's never enough.

Jill Norris

Natural Processes and Hazards

Project

Choose one of the project options below.

Option 1: Earthquake Sensor Chimes

Wind chimes are often hung outside as a pleasant-sounding decoration. When the air moves even just a little, the pieces of the chimes tap each other. You can use chimes to sense an earthquake, too. Gather items that make a sound when they tap. Metal and glass objects work well, although thin glass can break easily. After you have objects that will make noise together, use thread, fishing line, or dental floss and tie to attach them to a top piece. The objects need to hang freely so they can move if there are vibrations in the ground. When your chimes are complete, hang them from the ceiling, on a wall, or in an open doorway indoors. Even when the ground is still, you have a pretty piece of art to look at.

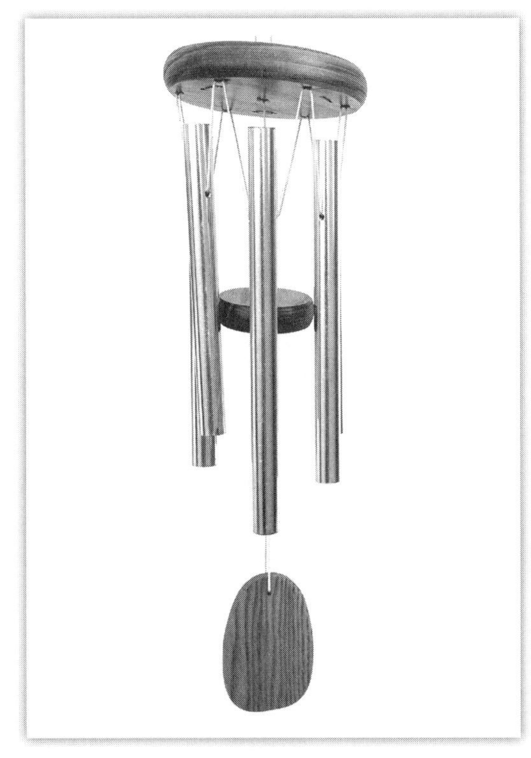

Option 2: Get to Safety Video or Poster

Choose a hazard that affects your area. It might be a weather event, such as a hurricane, tornado, flood, or forest fire caused by lightning. It could be something caused by ground movement, such as a volcano or an earthquake. Then find out a plan that your school, home, or community uses when this hazard occurs. Create a video or poster that shows exactly what to do and how to do it safely. It should also explain why you do each thing.

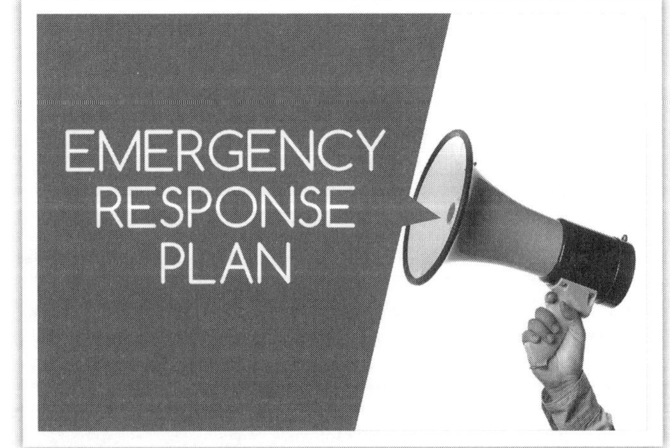

Physical Science: Changes in Movement

Concept

Forces and Motion: Each force acts on one particular object and has both strength and a direction. Forces can cause changes in the object's speed or direction of motion. Objects at rest have multiple forces acting on them that cancel each other out.

Lesson Objectives

- Students will explore forces that make things move, change direction, and stop.
- Students will identify when forces acting on an object are balanced or unbalanced.
- Students will investigate how friction, air resistance, and gravity change movement.

Learning Approach

The learning path in this unit is designed to take students through different phases of learning based on the 5E model. This approach allows students to explore and connect to an idea through relatable activities, to build on prior knowledge and experience, to construct meaning, and to use or apply their understanding of a concept in a creative way.

Teacher Resource Page

Student Pages

Engage

Changes in Movement

Introduce the Concept

Distribute or display the unit concept page to students and ask them to think about their experiences making objects move, change direction, or stop. Read the Spark Question and ask students to think about it. Next, use the text in the Discussion Guide (read it or paraphrase it) to facilitate a conversation that encourages students to share their experiences with tops. Use Think-Pair-Share, a whole-class discussion, or any other format that suits your class.

Spark Question

Why does a top stop spinning?

Discussion Guide: Spinning Tops

Children have played with spinning tops for thousands of years. Tops come in all shapes, sizes, and colors. They are made out of plastic, wood, or metal. A dreidel is a four-sided top used during Hanukkah, a Jewish holiday. Have you ever played with a top or a dreidel?

With a simple flick of your fingers, you can make a top spin. A top spins round and round as it moves across the floor. Can a top stand on its own? What happens if you try to make it stand up without spinning it? What are some other items that spin? What objects move in ways besides spinning? In this unit, you will explore how things move and what makes their movement change.

Explore Activity Preparation

Spinning Top Exploration: Students will need an uncluttered desktop or open floor space for this activity. If you want to restrict each pair's space, you can provide trays or cardboard box lids with a raised edge or plastic bins for students to use.

Students will need to know how to use a timer. Give them instruction and practice starting, stopping, and reading the timer.

Engage

Changes in Movement

Explore

Changes in Movement

Spinning Top Exploration

You will work in pairs to explore spinning tops.

What You'll Need

- a top
- a timer
- a pencil

What You'll Do

1. Work with your partner to become familiar with your top. Give your top a "twist push" to start it spinning. Watch your top's movement. Pay attention to its speed. Does it hit anything? What happens before it stops?

2. Once you and your partner have had several turns spinning the top, you are ready to collect some data. You will be timing how long the top spins. First, decide with your partner how you will know when the top has stopped spinning. What will the top look like at that moment? Complete the statement at the top of the next page.

3. Make sure that you and your partner agree on how you will know when the top has stopped spinning. What will the top be doing once it has stopped spinning?

4. Take turns spinning the top and using the timer to find out how long it spins each time, using the statement you wrote. Spin the top a total of four times. Time how long it takes the top to stop spinning, and record each time in the table on the next page.

5. Then work with your partner to answer the questions.

Changes in Movement

Data and Observations

Name ______________________

The top has stopped when ____

____.

Spin Number	How long did it take the top to stop spinning?
1	
2	
3	
4	

1. Describe your top's movement. Write everything you notice.

____

____

2. What was the longest amount of time you got the top to spin? ______________
   What do you think helped the top spin for so long?

____

____

Preliminary Prediction

3. How does the top's movement change just before it stops?

____

____

4. Why do you think the top stops?

____

____

Changes in Movement

Move the Marble Exploration

You will work in groups of four to move a marble in a game.

What You'll Need

- a large sheet of butcher paper
- markers
- a marble
- 4 straws

What You'll Do

1. Use the markers to draw a simple maze on your butcher paper. The maze must have a Start and an End. It must also have at least 3 curves or corners in the path between the Start and End.
2. All four group members work together to move the marble from the Start to the End. Follow these rules:
   - Place the marble at the Start.
   - Move the marble along the path to get to the End.
   - You may
     - blow on the marble with the straw and
     - pick up the edge of the paper.
   - You may not touch the marble to move it along the path or to keep it from leaving the path.
   - If the marble rolls outside the path, you must place it back at the Start and try again.
3. After your group moves the marble to the End, answer the questions on the next page.

Explore

Changes in Movement

Observations

Name ______________________________

1. Describe different ways you tried to move the marble.

____

____

2. What did you do that was least successful? ______________________________
   Why do you think it didn't work?

____

3. What did you do that was most successful? ______________________________
   Why do you think it worked so well?

____

4. How did your group work together to move the marble?

____

____

____

Preliminary Explanation

5. What kinds of forces made the marble move?

____

6. What kinds of forces made the marble change direction?

____

7. What kinds of forces made the marble stop?

____

Changes in Movement

A World of Forces

What makes a rocket launch into the sky or a roller coaster speed down a hill? Forces make things move. A force is a push or a pull. You cannot see a force, but you can see what it does. A pull lifts up a glass of water. A push against the ground makes a skateboarder glide away.

When you think of forces, you probably think of making objects move. But sometimes they make things stop moving. If you bumped an egg on the kitchen counter, the egg would start to roll. If you use an equal force against the rolling egg, you can stop its movement before it falls to the floor. When a force stops an equal force, those forces are **balanced**. The object does not move. When the forces are **unbalanced**, or not equal, the object moves. Say you are standing still. Then your dog jumps up on you. The dog is using more force, and it makes you move.

A force has both **strength** and **direction**. Think about shooting a basketball toward a hoop. You must throw the ball with enough strength. If the force is not strong enough, the ball will not reach the hoop. You must also aim in the direction of the hoop. If your aim is off, the ball will miss. Some forces affect, or change, the way something is moving. A force can slow down movement or speed it up. How fast or slow an object goes depends on the force's strength. A force can also make a moving object change direction. It can even change an object's shape.

speed up

slow down

Jordan Tan / Shutterstock.com

change direction

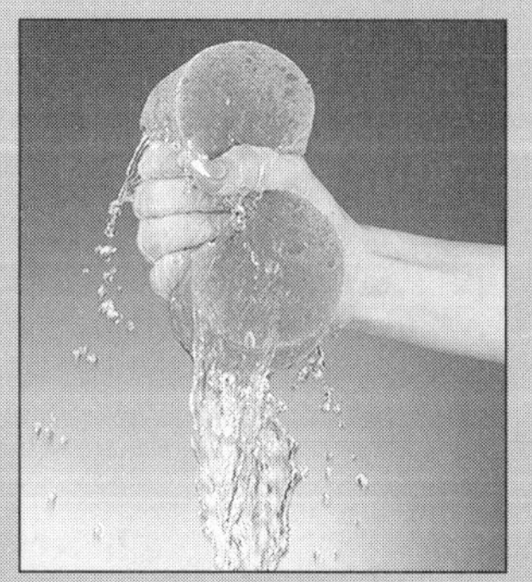
change shape

You can see a person pushing a shopping cart or a tow truck pulling a car. You can see a tree falling onto a fence or a volcano spitting lava up into the air. But some forces are not as noticeable.

Gravity is a force that pulls objects toward each other. Gravity is at work all the time, although you can see it only when an object is falling. Gravity pulls you and everything else on Earth in one direction—down toward Earth's center.

Friction is a force between objects that are touching. When **surfaces** touch, they rub together. This slows down movement. Try swinging your foot through the air. Then rub it along the floor. It doesn't move quite as fast or as easily. Imagine a sled going down a hill. If the sled is on snow, it will slide easily and quickly. If the sled is on grass or dirt, it will slide a bit more slowly. These surfaces are not as smooth as snow. They have more friction, which slows down the sled. Now imagine a sled going down gravel. Gravel is such a rough surface that the sled might just stop—that's a lot of friction!

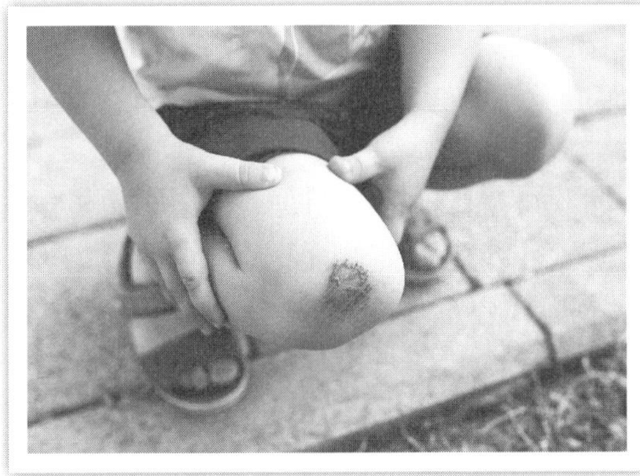

This child skinned his knee when he tripped and fell on the brick patio. The friction between his skin and the rough surface scraped off some skin.

Air also creates friction and slows down objects. Drop a piece of notebook paper. Do you see how the air under the paper slows the paper's fall? This type of friction is called **air resistance**. When you ride your bike fast, do you feel air blowing on your face, making your hair move? That's air resistance, too. Imagine how much faster you could ride if air resistance weren't slowing you down! We may not see forces doing their job, but they're at work all around us.

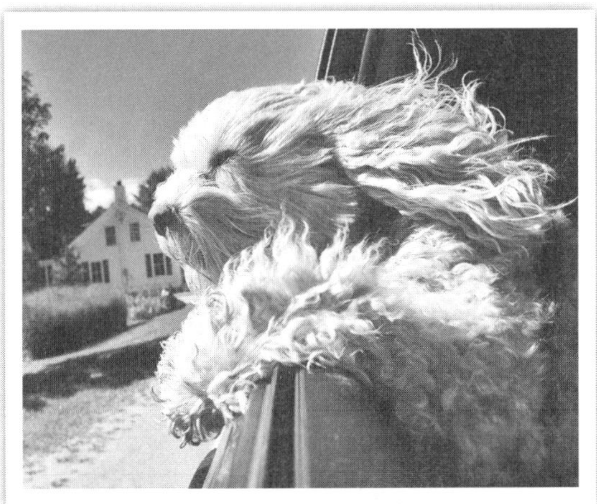

The fur on this dog's face, ears, and paws is blown backward as the car moves down the road.

Explain

Changes in Movement

Concept Vocabulary

air resistance:
a force that slows down an object as it moves against or through air

balanced forces:
equal forces working against each other

direction:
which way something travels

friction:
a force that slows down an object as it moves against another object

gravity:
a force that pulls all objects downward toward the center of Earth

strength:
the amount of power a force has

surface:
the top layer

unbalanced forces:
forces that are not equal or are not working against each other

Notes

Evaluate

Changes in Movement

Vocabulary Review

Name ______________________________

1. Imagine a bowling pin with balanced forces working on it. Now imagine unbalanced forces working on it. What difference would you see?

____

____

2. Look at the bicycle racer. Which of these is slowing him down? Circle it.

gravity   air resistance   unbalanced forces

Complete the sentences using terms from the Concept Vocabulary page.

3. I would move faster on a shiny metal slide than on an old rusty slide because of ____________________.

4. To go higher on a swing, the push needs more ____________________.

5. If you drop a coin, ____________________ will pull it down to Earth's ____________________.

6. Look at the picture of the man on his cellphone. To avoid falling into the hole, the man needs to change ____________________.

Evaluate

Changes in Movement

Concept Comprehension

Name ____________________

1. Look at each photo. Write **push** or **pull** to describe the force being used.

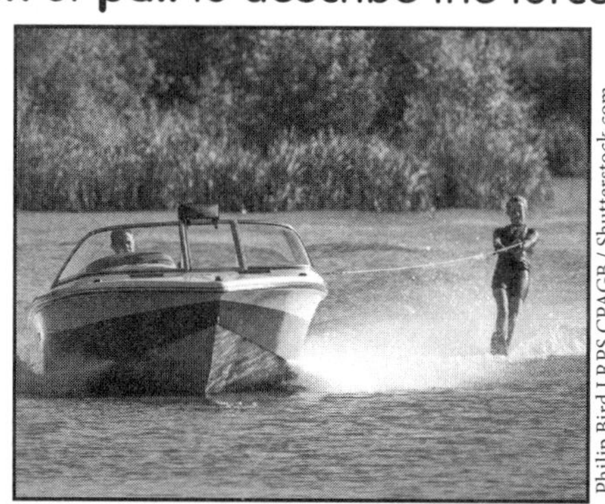

Philip Bird LRPS CPAGB / Shutterstock.com

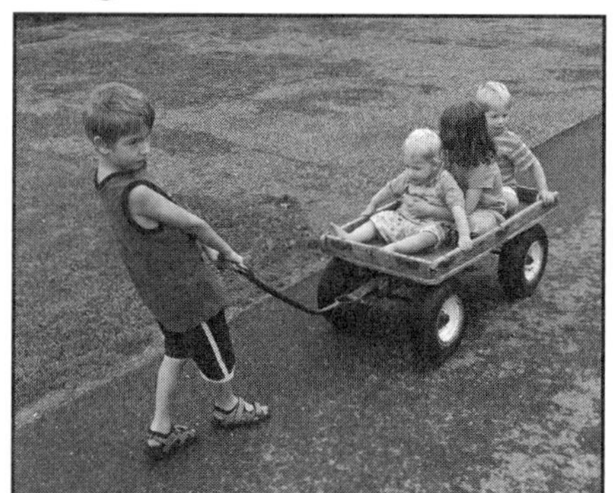

____________ ____________ ____________

2. Scientists use diagrams to show where forces are. Arrows in the diagrams show the direction of the forces. The longer the arrow, the stronger the force. In the diagrams below, forces affect the movement of a box.

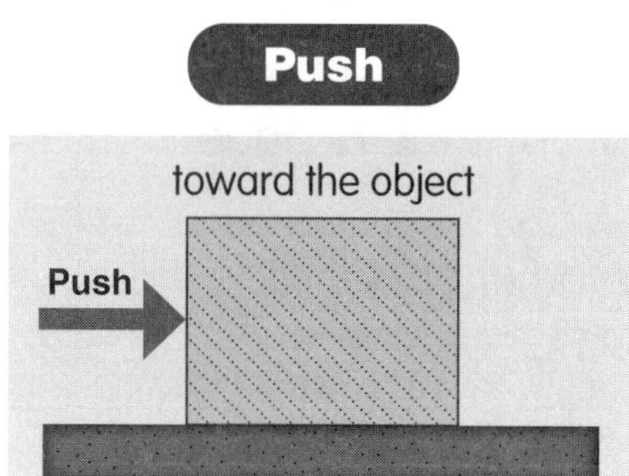

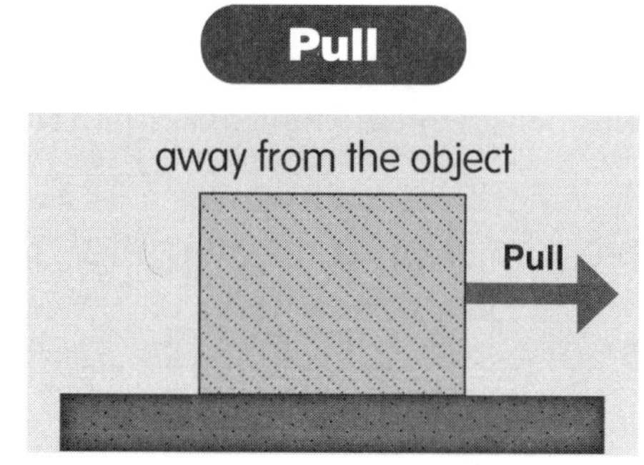

Now look at the diagrams below. In the box, write **B** if the forces are balanced. Write **U** if the forces are unbalanced.

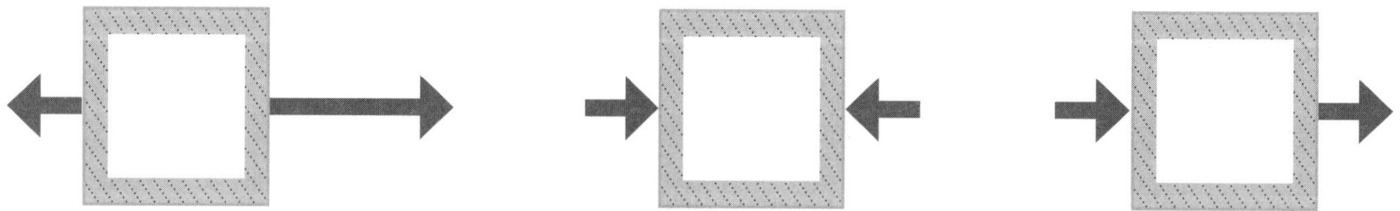

3. Rolling out dough shows that force can ________.

slow movement down   change an object's shape   pull downward

4. Does the force of gravity make objects move or slow down objects?

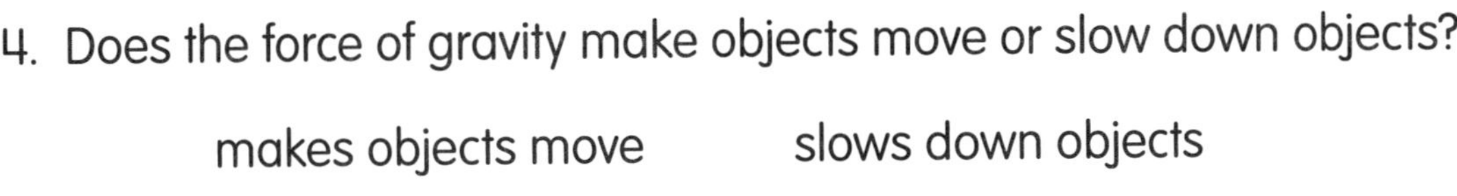

makes objects move   slows down objects

Explain your answer.

____

____

5. Pretend you are making a bookshelf. You want the books to stay in place, not slide around when someone takes a book off the shelf. What material would you use on the surface where the books sit to prevent sliding? Explain your choice.

____

____

____

6. Look at the picture of a playground. Draw a circle around two examples of balanced forces. Draw a box around two examples of unbalanced forces. Then write one place where you see each of these three forces:

gravity

____

friction

____

air resistance

____

Extend

Changes in Movement

Reflect

Name ____________________

Draw a diagram of a spinning top. Use words and arrows to show the forces that are affecting the top. Then write how each of the forces you wrote affects the top's movement.

Spinning Top Diagram

Extend

Changes in Movement

Imagine

Name ______________________________

Imagine that you jump from a plane wearing a parachute. Your parachute opens and you land safely on the ground.

Write a paragraph about your jump. Describe the forces affecting you and your parachute.

Extend

Changes in Movement

Project

Choose one of the project options below.

Option 1: Create Your Own Top

Design and create your own spinning top using materials you collect from school or home. Use some of these materials: CDs, pencils, paper clips, tape, bottle caps, pushpins, toothpicks, paper, and marbles. Glue the materials together. Once your top will spin, decorate it and spin it some more.

Option 2: Video Dictionary

Use a camera or a smartphone to take photographs or a video of some of the ways children use forces on the playground. Narrate your video or write a script to go with the video. Use vocabulary from this unit.

Plan Your Project

Physical Science: Predicting Motion from Patterns

Concept

Forces and Motion: The patterns of an object's motion can be measured and used to predict future motion.

Lesson Objectives

- Students identify, describe, and measure patterns in motion.
- Students predict future action and take advantage of it.

Learning Approach

The learning path in this unit is designed to take students through different phases of learning based on the 5E model. This approach allows students to explore and connect to an idea through relatable activities, to build on prior knowledge and experience, to construct meaning, and to use or apply their understanding of a concept in a creative way.

Teacher Resource Page

Student Pages

Engage

Predicting Motion from Patterns

Introduce the Concept

Distribute or display the unit concept page. Have students study the action in the photos. Read the Spark Question and ask students to think about it. Next, use the text in the Discussion Guide (read it or paraphrase it) to facilitate a conversation that encourages students to describe a variety of patterns of motion (back and forth, up and down, in a circle, forward, backward, sideways, all at different speeds). Show short video clips of similar actions (bouncing ball, roller coaster going backward, trampoline, skydiver jumping and opening a parachute), stopping before the outcome and asking for predictions. Use Think-Pair-Share, a whole-class discussion, or any other format that suits your class.

Spark Question

How can you take a photo of a diver somersaulting in mid-air?

Discussion Guide: Capturing Action

Imagine that you have an older sister who competes in diving. She climbs up a ladder to a diving board high above the pool. She walks quickly to the edge of the board and jumps once on the end. Then she flips her body around quickly before heading into the water. You would love to take a photo of her dive. But how do you know just when to shoot the picture?

Look at the photos (and any videos) again. Describe the type of motion you see. How fast is the motion? Does the motion happen over and over without anything in between? Or are there other actions in between the repeated parts? How do you know what will happen next? Do any of the photos (or videos) show surprises? Choose a surprise and explain why you think it happened.

Explore Activity Preparation

Find an outdoor location, such as a playground or field, where students can safely run or walk fast. The location must have access to a water spigot. Find an oscillating impact or gear-drive sprinkler head on a flat base or stake. Attach the spigot, hose, and sprinkler. Adjust the sprinkler distance, pattern, and speed if possible. Set the sprinkler in or on the ground and test it. Determine starting and ending points that make a line through the sprinkler's range and mark the points for the students. In a notebook or on a clipboard, set up a class data table. Write your name on the first line and each student's name following.

Engage

Predicting Motion from Patterns

Explore

Predicting Motion from Patterns

Sprinkler Exploration

You will work with your class to figure out how to pass by a sprinkler and stay dry.

What You'll Need

- a large outdoor space
- a sprinkler
- a garden hose attached to a faucet
- a stopwatch
- a class data table
- a pencil
- bath towels

What You'll Do

1. Watch your teacher demonstrate how to use the stopwatch to time how long it takes to move from the starting point to the ending point. Start the stopwatch when someone starts moving forward from the starting point. Notice how your teacher records the time on the class data table.

2. One by one, each student moves from the starting point to the ending point past the sprinkler. Students go to the end of the line after their turn to wait for their next turn.
   - Watch the sprinkler's pattern of motion.
   - Watch your classmates move past the sprinkler.
   - Figure out a strategy to move past it and stay dry. You will have two or more turns, depending on how long your teacher gives you.

3. The next student in line uses the stopwatch to time how fast the student at the front of the line moves past the sprinkler and records the time on the class data table. The recording student gives the stopwatch, class data table, and pencil to the next student in line before taking his or her turn.

4. Once all students have completed their turns, return to the classroom to complete the next page.

Explore

Predicting Motion from Patterns

Data and Observations

Name________________________

1. Find your times on the class date table. Fill in the table below with your time for each turn and whether you stayed dry.

	1st turn	2nd turn	3rd turn	4th turn
Time (seconds)				
Did you stay dry?				

2. Compare your times with whether or not you stayed dry. Describe any pattern you see.

____

____

____

3. Describe the sprinkler's pattern of motion in detail. ________________________

____

____

Preliminary Explanation

4. Think about the turns in which you stayed dry or didn't get as wet. How would you explain to someone how to go past the sprinkler and stay dry?

____

____

____

____

Explain

Predicting Motion from Patterns

Motion Patterns All Around Us

Our brains like to find **patterns**. Patterns make things look nice. You can find pretty patterns in floor tiles, clothing, and decorations. Patterns make music sound nice. It's why songs are easy to learn. Patterns make it easier to get through your day. Your morning routine is a pattern that helps you get ready for school even if you are still sleepy. Patterns help us know what to expect. People, animals, and objects often behave in certain ways in certain situations. For example, your dog might wag its tail side to side to greet you when you come home every day, and it might always hide during a thunderstorm.

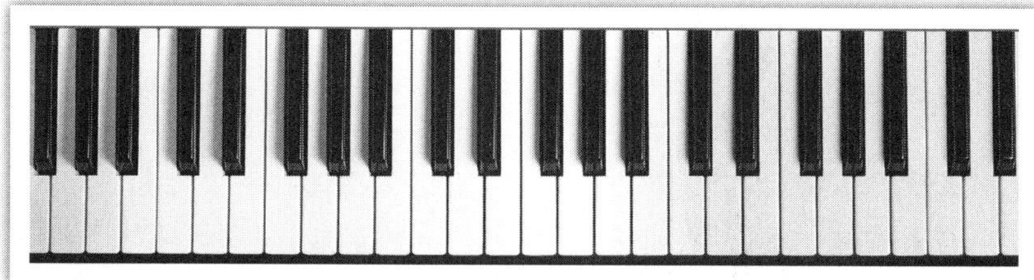

A piano has an arrangement of white keys and groups of black keys. Can you figure out where the pattern repeats?

A pattern is a design, action, behavior, movement, or arrangement that repeats. You have probably seen many patterns used in your home. Think about your furniture, floors, cabinets, picture frames, bedspread, and clothing. There are sound patterns in your home as well: the ringtone on your phone, a timer or clock alarm, a spoon stirring food in a pan in a **circular** motion, footsteps going up the stairs, a broom going back and forth over the floor. Actions cause those sounds.

The sweater has a pattern knitted into it.

The tiles make a pattern when they are put together on a wall.

When you play a sport, you make all kinds of **motion** patterns. In most sports, the players try to move a ball, puck, or another object forward into a goal. They hit, kick, or throw the object around the field or court, sometimes to their teammates. Often the force on the object moves it forward. A basketball is often bounced up and down as the player travels around the court. Then it travels in a curve toward the basket. Soccer players often tap the ball lightly from one foot to the other in a **zigzag** motion as they run down the field. In American football, the ball spins around in a **spiral** movement when one player throws it to another. The pattern of those movements helps you **predict** how the movements will continue. Correct predictions help a player be in the right place to move the object and score.

You can use predictions of motion to help you stay safe. If you walk behind a swing on the playground, you need to predict the swing's **pendulum** motion so that you are not hit by it. Watching the **speed** at which an escalator's stairs appear will help you get on at the right time without tripping or falling. Surfers must follow the pattern of a wave's motion to know the right moment to start riding it.

The pendulum of the clock swings back and forth on a curve.

Some activities involve predicting motion. To jump rope, you need to know when the rope is just about to reach your feet so you can jump or hop at just the right moment. A juggler needs to know how fast and where each object is falling so he or she can catch it.

Each step of the escalator rises out of the floor in a timed pattern.

Explain

Predicting Motion from Patterns

People aren't the only ones putting things in motion. Our planet turns around every 24 hours, making night and day. Can you predict how light it will be at 8:00 tonight? If an apple falls off a branch, can you predict what will happen to it? If you see ocean waves heading for the shore, can you predict when your feet will get wet?

Animals in nature move predictably, too. The black mamba snake in Africa can move faster than a human can run! It uses **serpentine** movement to slither away from danger. It makes S-shaped curves, pushing off of rough spots on the ground. Other snakes move like a caterpillar, which hunches the back part of its body up into a small curve that goes up and down. Then it pulls the front part of its body forward as it pushes the curve down.

The black mamba snake curves side to side to move forward, while the caterpillar curves its body up and down to move forward.

black mamba snake

caterpillar

Objects not only move in patterns, but they also *stop* moving in patterns. If you drop a rubber ball and don't touch it again, each bounce comes up lower than the one before it. Finally it stops. The same thing happens to a swing once someone jumps off. It will go back and forth a shorter distance each time until it stops.

If you know how something moves, you can use it to your advantage!

Explain

Predicting Motion from Patterns

Concept Vocabulary

circular:
movement around in a circle shape

motion:
movement, action

pattern:
a design, action, behavior, movement, or arrangement that happens over and over

pendulum:
an object hanging down that can swing freely back and forth on a curve

predict:
to say what will probably happen

serpentine:
a wiggly back-and-forth movement in an S-shape

speed:
how fast something moves

spiral:
movement that goes round and round as it moves away from its starting point

zigzag:
forward movement that keeps changing direction back and forth

Notes

Evaluate

Predicting Motion from Patterns

Vocabulary Review

Name ____________________

1. Complete the model for the term **pendulum**.

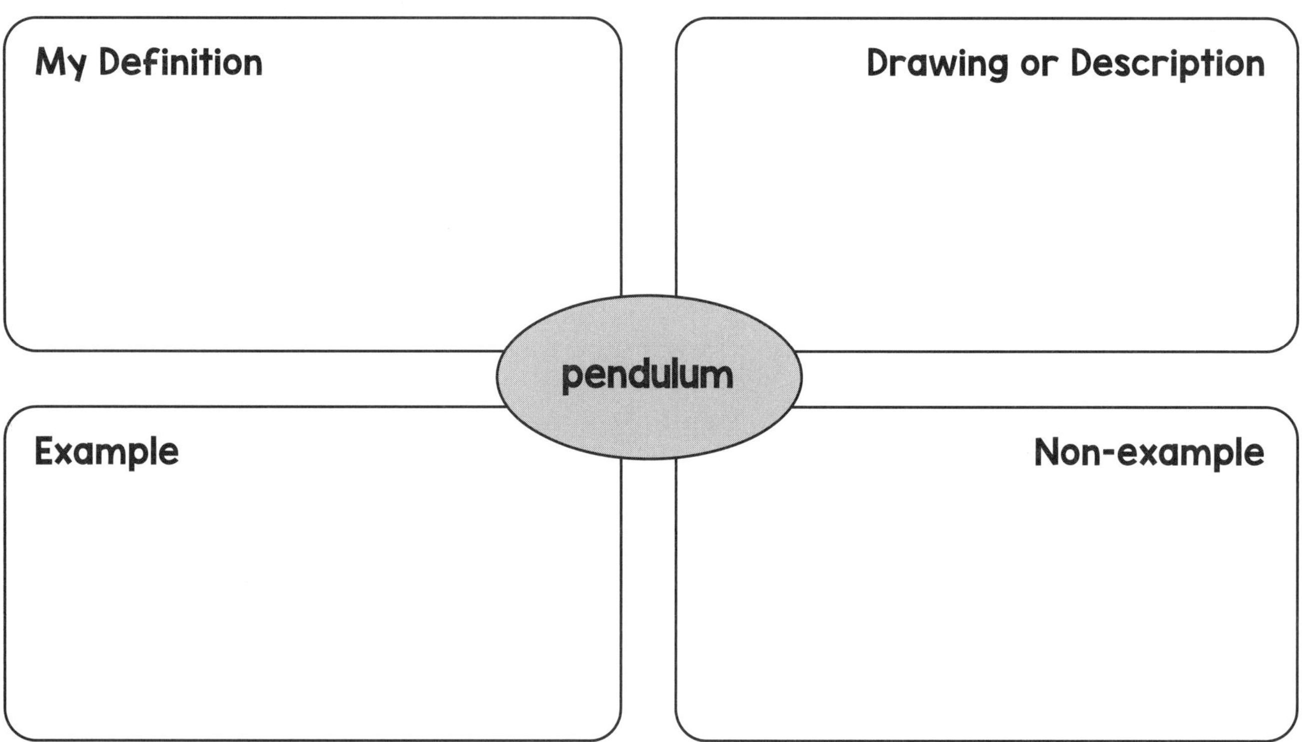

2. Complete the paragraph using terms from the Concept Vocabulary page.

The room was silent as Joy stared at the two bowling pins at the end of the lane. The pins were far apart. This was her last throw of the competition. It would decide the winner. She thought about the exact ________________ she would need to make both pins fall. Joy started her familiar ________________ of movement. She breathed in deeply as she brought the ball up in front of her body. Then she swung her arm back as she took four steps. As her arm came forward, she carefully released the ball. Everyone held their breath as they ________________ whether the ball would knock down both pins.

Evaluate

Predicting Motion from Patterns

3. Draw an animal or an object moving in each pattern.

circular	spiral
serpentine	zigzag

4. How are the circular and spiral movements similar and different?

   similar: ______________________________

   different: ______________________________

   ____

5. How are the serpentine and zigzag movements similar and different?

   similar: ______________________________

   different: ______________________________

   ____

Evaluate

Predicting Motion from Patterns

Concept Comprehension

Name ______________________________

1. Look at the photo of a tennis player about to hit a ball. Predict the player's motion and the ball's motion. Describe both.

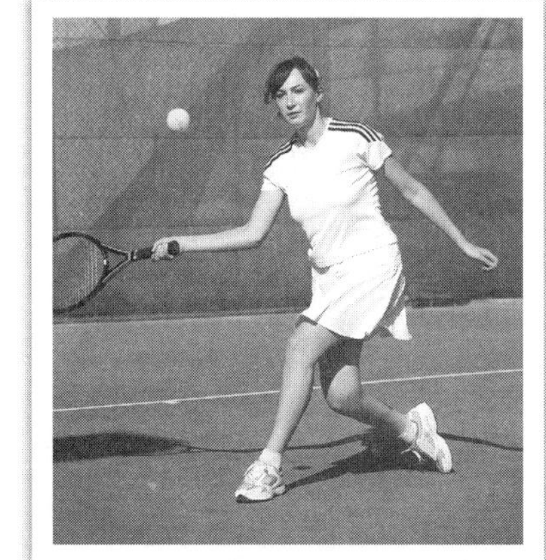

____

____

____

____

2. You come to a stoplight walking home from school. You press a button to stop the cars so you can cross the street safely. The light changes and you see the "walk" symbol. The symbol blinks as it counts down from 20. What pattern do you see? How will it help you cross safely?

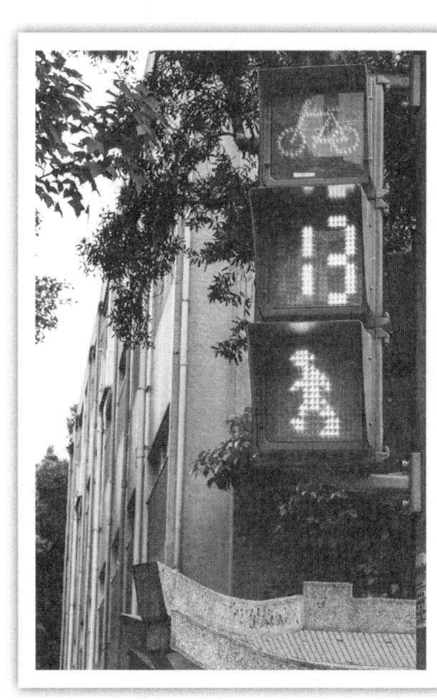

____

____

____

____

____

3. Write the name of a team sport that uses a pattern of motion. ______________

Describe one pattern's direction and speed. ______________________

____

____

How do players use this pattern to help them play the game? ______________

____

Evaluate

Predicting Motion from Patterns

4. When Mr. Ogren's students came back from lunch, Sam noticed that Sally Snail, the class pet, had crawled out of her box. Think about a snail's pattern of movement. Where should Sam start looking for Sally?

___

___

5. The weather forecast calls for strong winds to blow toward the west tonight. Here is Kemi's yard. Predict how it will look when the winds are blowing. Draw how the yard will look after the winds blow.

After

6. Ravi just jumped off the swing as it swung forward. Draw the next four movements of the empty swing.

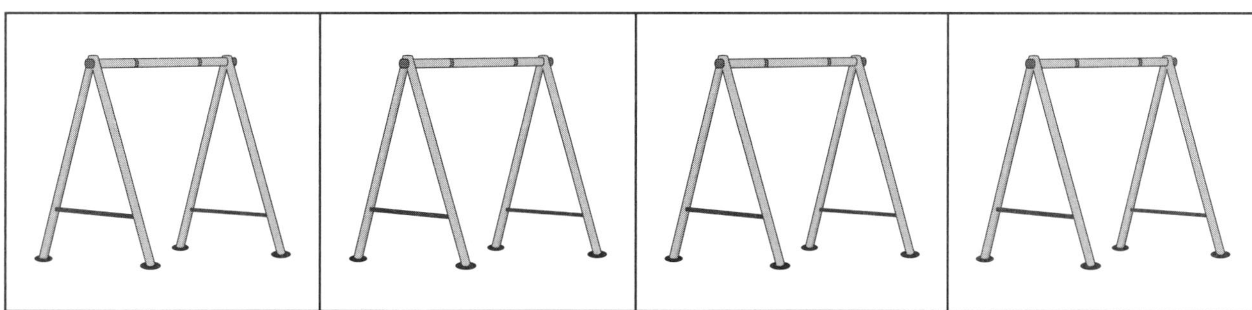

Predicting Motion from Patterns

Analyze

Name 

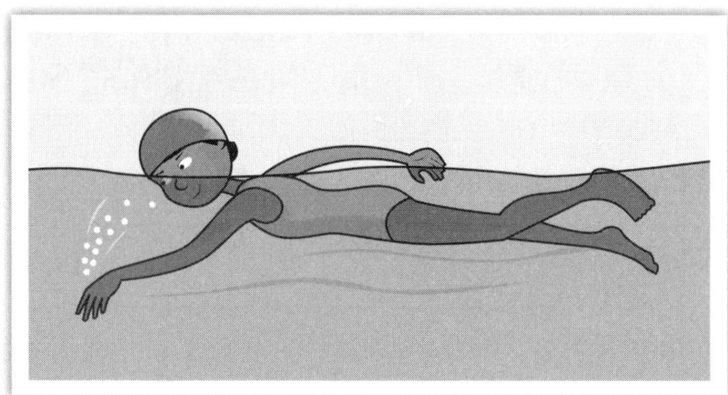

Think of how a swimmer moves, or watch a video of someone swimming. Imagine that you are seeing the swimmer move in slow motion. Break down all the different parts of the movement. Write a description of what the swimmer does. What type of motion is each body part doing? How fast are the movements? Are they all the same speed? If the swimmer continues for several minutes, what prediction could you make about where the swimmer will be and how fast the movements will be?

The swimmer's arms ______________________________

____

____

______________________________.

The swimmer's legs ______________________________

____

____

______________________________.

In several minutes, the swimmer ______________________________

____

____

____

______________________________.

Extend

Predicting Motion from Patterns

Invent

Name ______________________________

Imagine that you are a sports reporter. You are describing a competition or a game. Invent symbols to represent motion patterns that happen in the sport or game. Then use them to write a paragraph about an exciting play in the sport or game you are watching.

Example:

circular

The figure skater tucked in his arms and spun  quickly 8 times.

Symbols:

____

____

____

____

____

____

____

____

____

____

Extend

Predicting Motion from Patterns

Project

Choose one of the project options below.

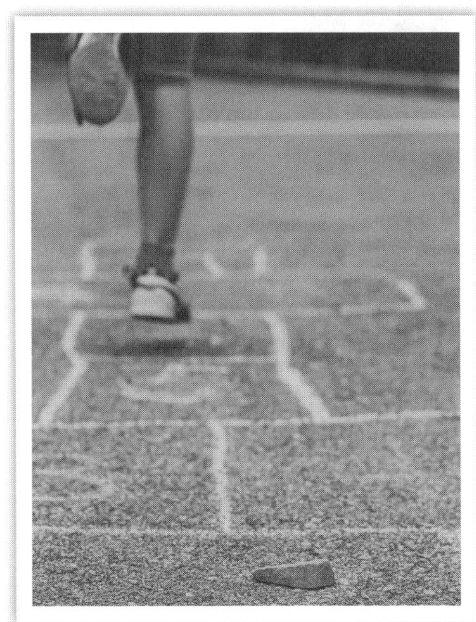

Option 1: Video Dictionary

Make a video using video clips of each of the motion patterns you learned about—forward, backward, back and forth, up and down, circular, zigzag, and serpentine. The motions can be made by people, animals, nature, or objects. Label each motion pattern. You can make or find the video clips. Write down the source of any online clips you use.

Option 2: Motion Design Art Show

Set up a sand pendulum. Find a large cardboard box lid. Place two chairs on opposite sides of the lid and set a broom or another long, solid object across the chairs. Fill the lid with a layer of dry sand, about 2 inches (5 centimeters) deep. To make the pendulum, tie a pencil, pen, or pair of scissors onto a long piece of string with the pointy end away from the string. Tie the other end of the string to the object hanging over the lid. Make sure that the pointy end goes into the sand but does not touch the bottom of the lid.

Pull the pendulum back a little and release it. Watch the pattern it draws in the sand, and photograph the design when the pendulum stops moving. Try starting from different heights, and experiment with gently pushing it on a curve to start. Photograph each result and display them.

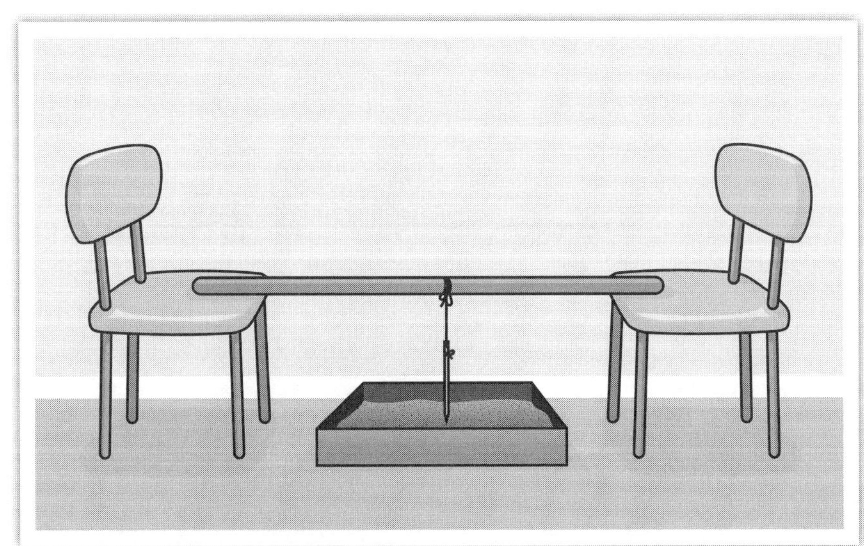

Physical Science: Magnetic Forces

Concept

Types of Interactions: Objects exert forces on each other. Magnetic forces do not require that the objects be in contact. The sizes of the magnetic forces in each situation depend on the properties of the objects and their distances apart and on their orientation relative to each other.

Lesson Objectives

- Students will distinguish between objects that a magnet will and will not attract and repel.
- Students will investigate the different strengths of magnets.

Learning Approach

The learning path in this unit is designed to take students through different phases of learning based on the 5E model. This approach allows students to explore and connect to an idea through relatable activities, to build on prior knowledge and experience, to construct meaning, and to use or apply their understanding of a concept in a creative way.

Teacher Resource Page

Student Pages

Engage

Magnetic Forces

Introduce the Concept

Distribute or display the unit concept page. Ask students to look at the photos and think about their experiences with magnets and ways people use magnets. Then read the Spark Question and have them think about it. Next, use the text in the Discussion Guide (read it or paraphrase it) to facilitate a conversation that encourages students to share what they know about magnets. Use Think-Pair-Share, a whole-class discussion, or any other format that suits your class.

Spark Question

Why do some magnets work better than others?

Discussion Guide: The Strength of Magnets

People use magnets in many ways. Where are magnets used in your home? What are they used for? What about in our classroom? Magnets help store information in computers. They help keep our refrigerator and cabinet doors latched, and they power speakers. They are used to code information in strips on the backs of credit cards. Magnets are used in many machines and motors, so think of something that uses a motor. Can you name any machines that might use a magnet? Strong magnets are used to separate metals in junkyards and in magnetic scanners that doctors use to see inside people's bodies. Even Earth itself is a large magnet. In this unit, you will explore objects that magnets attract and do not attract. You will also explore how strong magnets can be.

Explore Activity Preparation

Magnet Attraction Observation: Collect objects that magnets attract and do not attract. Suggested objects: paper clips, binder clips, staples, washers, stainless steel utensils, scissors, and other magnets. Also collect some objects that magnets will not attract, such as rubber bands, pennies, dimes, quarters, and objects made of glass, wood, plastic, or paper. Make an equal set of objects for each group of students, along with two strong magnets.

Magnet Strength Investigation: You will need magnets of different shapes and strengths. Make an equal set for each group of students. Each group will also need a box of 100 paper clips (all the same size).

Magnetic Forces

Explore

Magnetic Forces

Magnet Attraction Observation

You will work in small groups to explore what objects are attracted to magnets.

What You'll Need

- two strong magnets
- a variety of different objects
- a pencil

What You'll Do

1. Work with your group to explore magnets and test which objects a magnet attracts. Try different magnets with each object. Explore how magnets react to each other, too.
2. Write down the name of each object you test in the table on the next page.
3. Next to the name of each object, write **yes** if the object was attracted to a magnet. Write **no** if the object was not attracted to a magnet.
4. Then answer the questions on the next page.

Explore

Magnetic Forces

Data

Name ______________________

Name of object tested	Did a magnet attract the object?

1. Look at the objects that a magnet attracted. What do they have in common?

____

____

____

2. Did a magnet ever make an object move without touching it? Describe what you observed.

____

____

____

3. Did you ever feel two magnets repel, or push away from one another? How did it feel?

____

____

Explore

Magnetic Forces

Magnet Strength Investigation

You will work in small groups to measure the strengths of different magnets.

What You'll Need

- three or four different types or sizes of magnets
- a box of 100 paper clips
- a pencil

What You'll Do

1. Work with your group to measure the strength of your magnets. Each person in your group will test every magnet. You will need to take turns.
2. Select a magnet to test first. Draw the magnet in the table on the next page.
3. Place the magnet in the box of paper clips. Lift the magnet out and count how many paper clips are attached to the magnet.
4. Record your data in the table.
5. Put the paper clips back in the box.
6. Allow everyone in your group to have a turn testing the first magnet.
7. Repeat the steps above for each of the magnets.
8. Then answer the questions on the next page.

Explore

Magnetic Forces

Data

Name ______________________

Draw the magnet	Number of paper clips

Draw the magnet	Number of paper clips

Preliminary Hypothesis

1. Describe the size, shape, and weight of the strongest and weakest magnets.

___

___

2. How did you decide which ones were the strongest and weakest?

___

___

3. Imagine a magnet that could attract twice as many paper clips as your strongest magnet did. Describe the shape, size, and weight of your imaginary magnet.

___

___

Magnetic Forces

Amazing Magnets

When you bring home a work of art that you painted or a nice poem that you wrote at school, is it displayed on the refrigerator door? How is it attached? Chances are a magnet is involved.

Magnets pull, or **attract**, some kinds of metal. A magnet will not attract glass, plastic, wood, or anything else that does not contain metal. Magnets inside the refrigerator are what keep the door closed. A metal refrigerator door is attracted to magnets. That's what makes magnets stick to the outside of the door. Metal objects stick to a magnet but not the same way they stick to tape.

Magnets attract objects made of metal, but not all metals. Magnets are made of a metal called **iron**. Magnets attract other objects made of iron. Some metals are mixtures of different types of metal. If iron is part of the mixture, a magnet will pull it. Coins or soda cans won't stick to a magnet. They are not made of iron or any other **magnetic** material.

Magnetism is a moving, invisible force. All magnets have a **magnetic field** that you cannot see. It's the area around the magnet where a force can affect magnetic material. The magnet does not need to touch the object to affect it. The object just has to be inside the magnet's magnetic field.

Magnets have two ends, or **poles**. The poles are the parts of the magnet where its force is the strongest. The force enters the

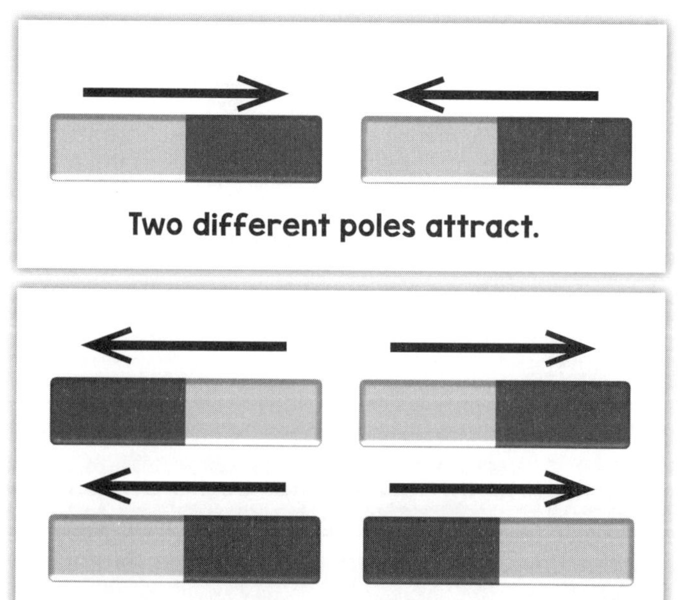

Two different poles attract.

Two of the same poles repel.

magnet at one pole and exits out the other pole. When two magnets are held with their entry and exit poles together, the poles attract each other and pull together. However, if two entry poles or two exit poles are held together, they **repel** one another, or push away.

All magnets are not created equal. Which magnets are stronger—big ones or small ones? You cannot know how strong a magnet is just by its size. The strength of a magnet has to do with its magnetic field. A strong magnetic field will attract more objects than a weaker magnetic field will. The stronger magnetic field will also attract objects that are farther away or that are heavier.

Look at these diagrams. The two magnets have different strengths. You cannot actually see the magnetic field, but the lines show where the field is. More lines mean more strength, so the magnet on the right is stronger than the one on the left.

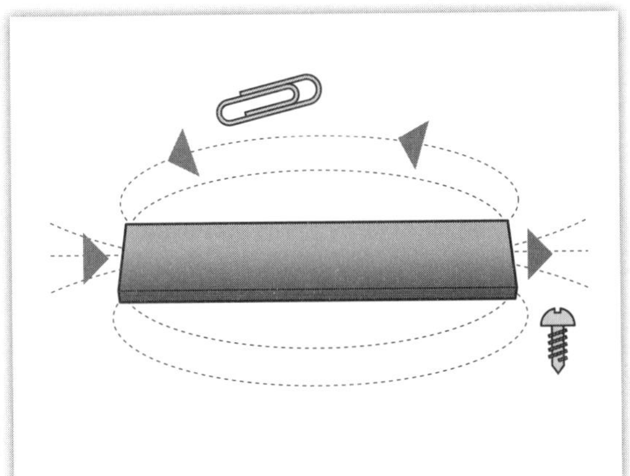

The paper clip and screw are just outside this magnet's field. The magnet will not move them.

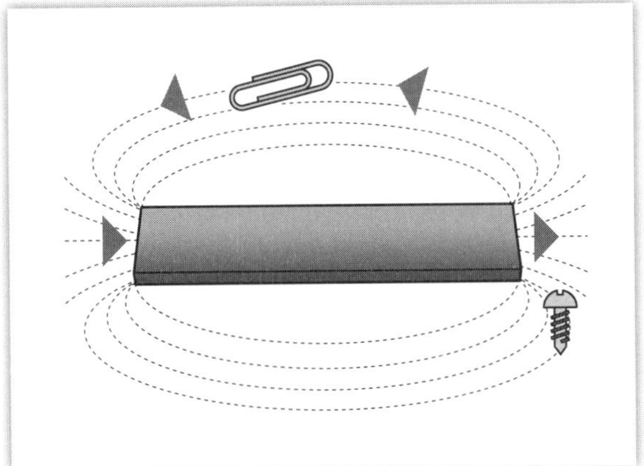

The paper clip and screw are within this magnet's field, so the magnet will pull them in.

The magnets on your refrigerator are a small example of magnets in action. They can be used to keep things closed, make things move, pick things up, separate things, and push things away. Whenever you spot these things happening, say, "I wonder if a magnet is doing the work."

Explain

Magnetic Forces

Concept Vocabulary

attract:
to pull toward something

iron:
a metal that is attracted to a magnet

magnetic:
able to attract iron or act like a magnet

magnetic field:
the space around a magnet where its force can be found

magnetism:
a force that attracts metal from a distance

pole:
either end or side of a magnet, where the magnetic force is strongest

repel:
to push away from something

Notes

Evaluate

Magnetic Forces

Vocabulary Review

Name ______________________________

1. Complete the model for the term **attract**.

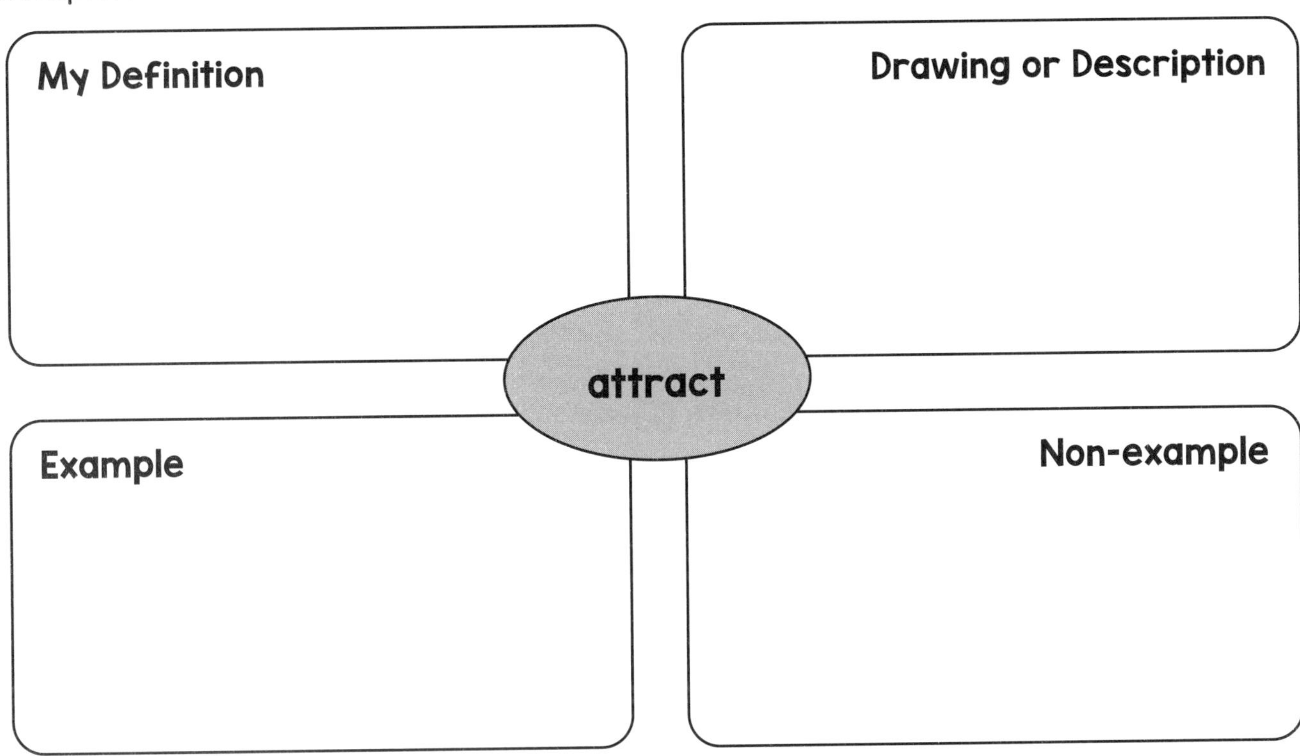

Complete the sentences using terms from the Concept Vocabulary page.

2. When the entry __________ of one magnet is near the entry __________ of another magnet, the magnets will ______________ one another.

3. A magnet pulls paper clips toward it because they have ______________ in them.

4. A magnet does not need to touch an object to pull it. As long as the object is in the ____________________ of a magnet, the magnet can pull the object.

5. Some people put ______________ letters on their refrigerators to spell words.

6. You can't see the force of ______________, but you can see it pull and push objects.

Magnetic Forces

Concept Comprehension

Name____________________

1. Draw an **X** on the objects that are not attracted to a magnet.

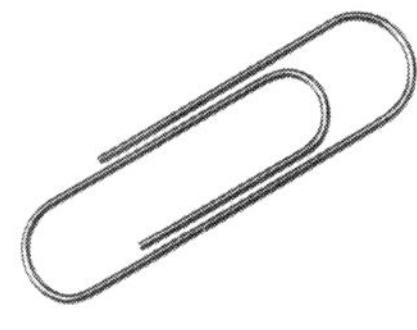

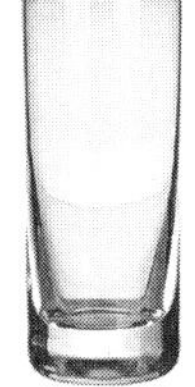
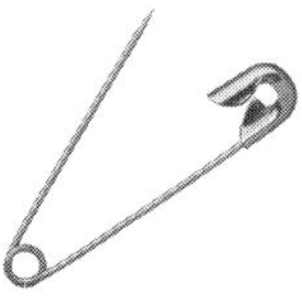

2. Which objects above may have iron in them? How could you test them?

____

____

____

Use the diagrams to answer questions 3 and 4.

3. Which diagram shows magnets that will attract? **A** **B**

4. Which diagram shows magnets that will repel? **A** **B**

5. Look at the magnets.

A

B

Which magnet has the greatest strength? **A** **B**

What is your evidence? I think it is the strongest magnet because

____.

6. Do you think a magnet's pull can go through paper? ____________

Explain your thinking.

____

____

7. Juan is experimenting with ring magnets. He placed one around a pencil with the exit side facing up. He is adding another magnet with the exit side facing down. When he lets go of the magnet, what do you think the magnets will do? Explain why.

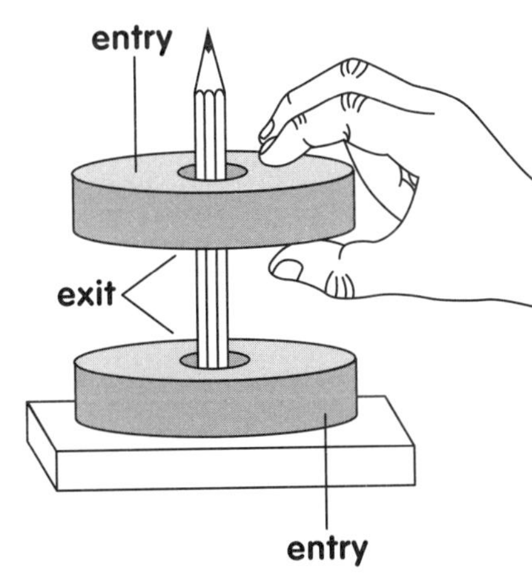

____

____

____

Magnetic Forces

Reflect

Name________________________________

Your teacher tries to hang a poster on a magnetic board using two magnets. The poster and magnets just slide down the board. The magnets just don't seem to stick. First, explain why the poster and magnets might slide down the board. Then explain what the teacher might be able to do to fix the problem.

Why the poster and magnets are sliding:

How to fix the problem:

Magnetic Forces

Invent

Name ____________________

Pretend that you are asked to invent a wooden toy car that you can move using the push or pull of magnets. Draw a diagram of the car you design. Label the poles of each magnet in your drawing. Use **S** to label the entry pole. Use **N** to label the exit pole. Draw an arrow to show which way your car will move. Then write a few sentences to explain how your car works.

My Magnetic Toy Car Diagram

Extend

Magnetic Forces

Project

Choose one of the project options below.

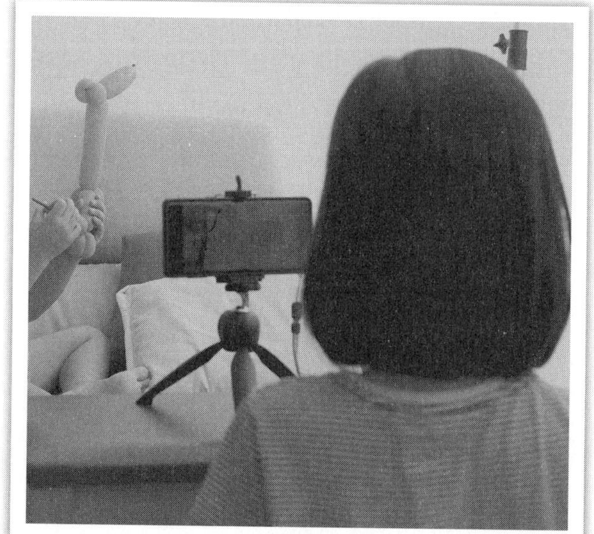

Option 1: Video Dictionary

A company that sells magnets wants a video to advertise its magnets on its website. The video should show different ways people use magnets. First, do some research on how people use magnets. Then use a camera or a smartphone to take photographs or videos of people using magnets. Narrate your video or write a script to go with the video. Use some of the vocabulary from this unit.

Option 2: Magnet Men

Gather a bunch of small magnetic hardware pieces (nuts, bolts, screws, nails, springs, wire, clips, etc.) and a variety of small magnets of different shapes. Use them to build figurines, robots, or animals. Create a scene with your magnet-and-hardware sculptures.

Answer Key

Page 18

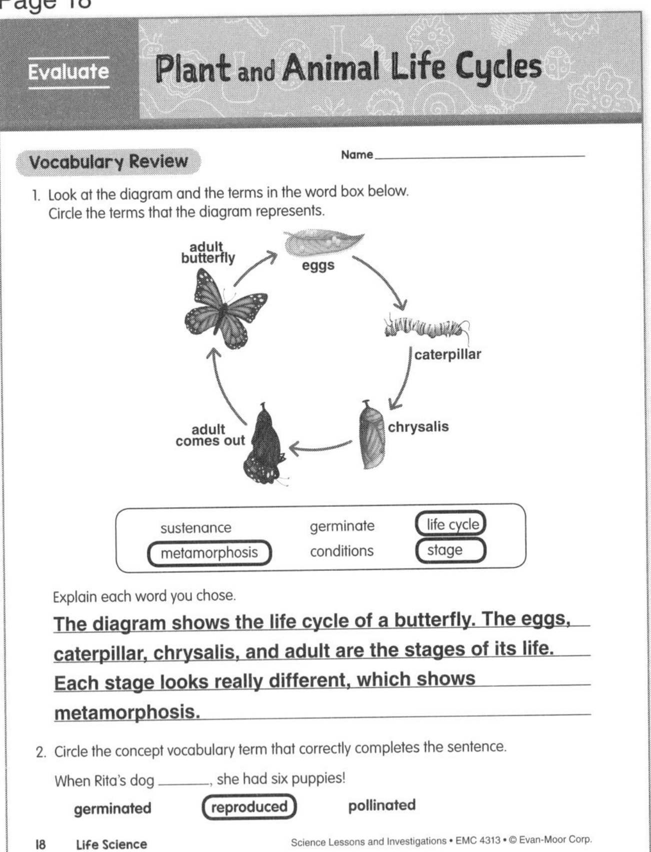

Page 19

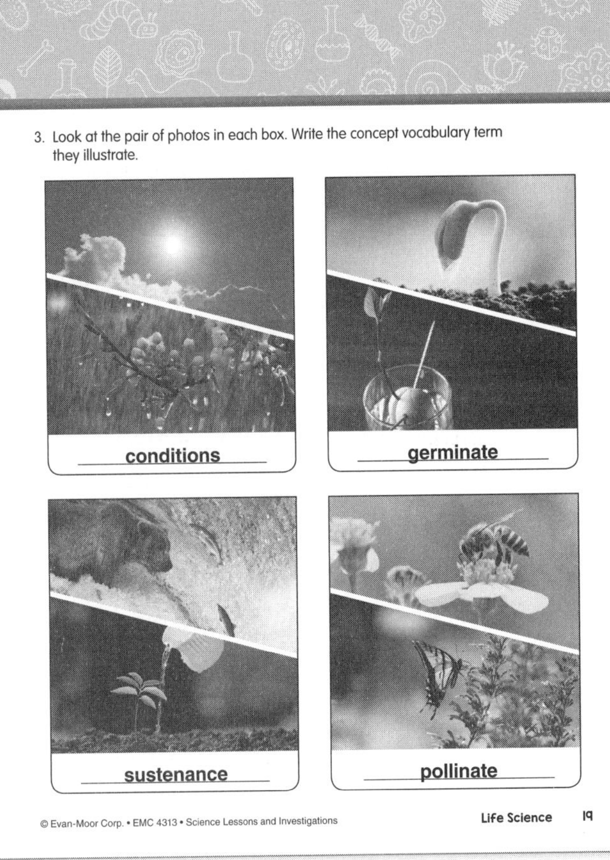

Page 20

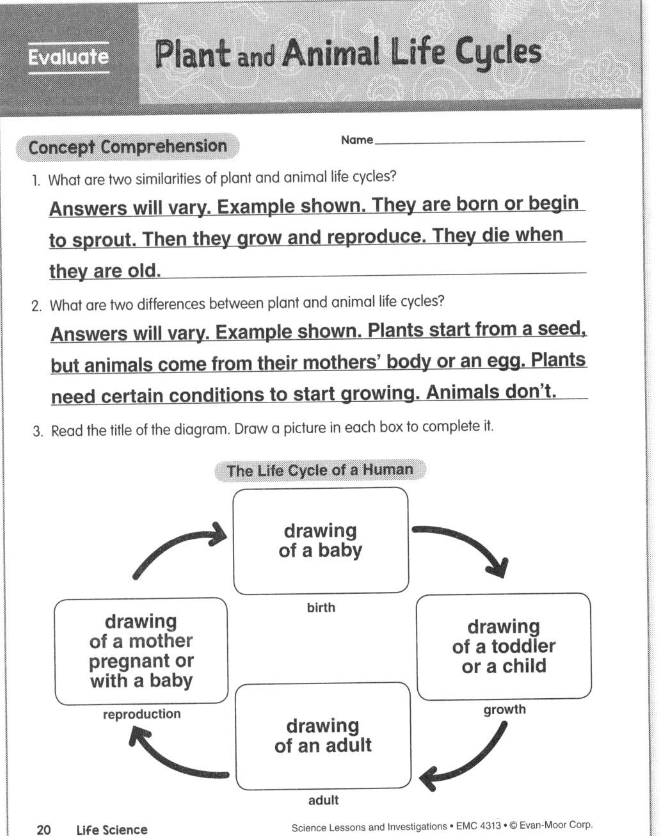

Page 21

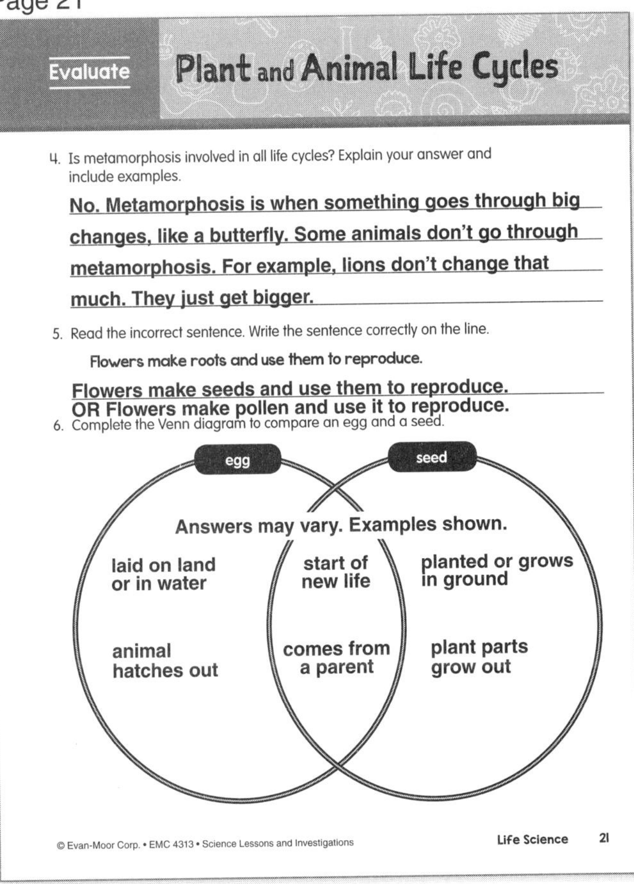

Page 35

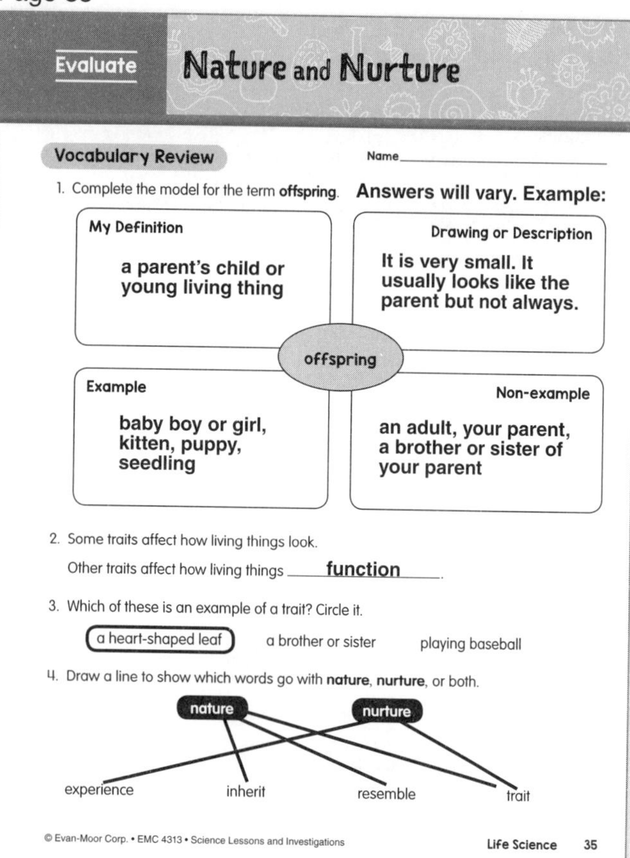

Evaluate — Nature and Nurture

Vocabulary Review Name___________

1. Complete the model for the term **offspring**. **Answers will vary. Example:**

My Definition	Drawing or Description
a parent's child or young living thing	**It is very small. It usually looks like the parent but not always.**

offspring

Example	Non-example
baby boy or girl, kitten, puppy, seedling	**an adult, your parent, a brother or sister of your parent**

2. Some traits affect how living things look.
   Other traits affect how living things **function**.
3. Which of these is an example of a trait? Circle it.
   (a heart-shaped leaf) a brother or sister playing baseball
4. Draw a line to show which words go with **nature**, **nurture**, or both.
   nature nurture
   experience inherit resemble trait

© Evan-Moor Corp. • EMC 4313 • Science Lessons and Investigations Life Science 35

Page 36

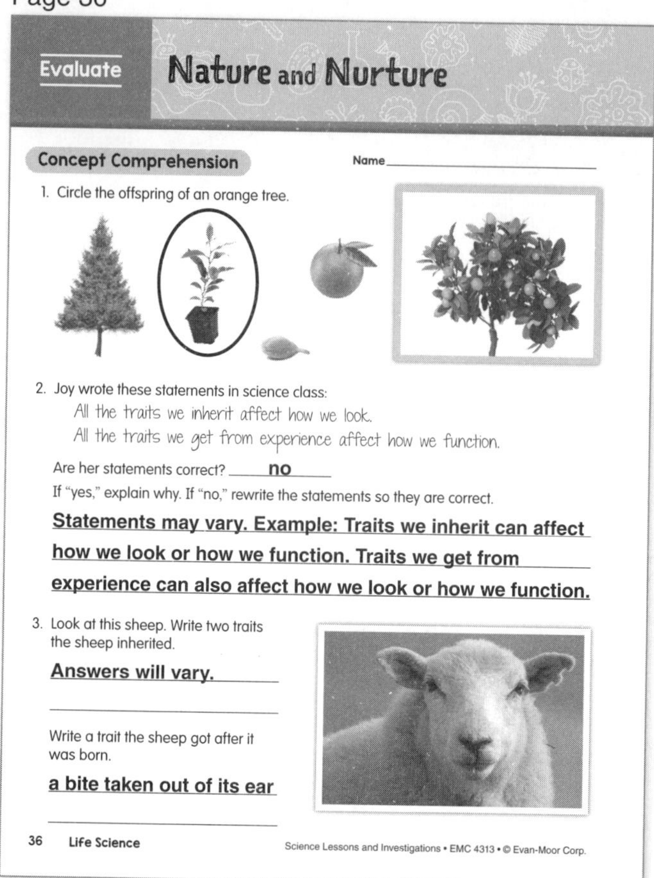

Evaluate — Nature and Nurture

Concept Comprehension Name___________

1. Circle the offspring of an orange tree.
2. Joy wrote these statements in science class:
   All the traits we inherit affect how we look.
   All the traits we get from experience affect how we function.
   Are her statements correct? **no**
   If "yes," explain why. If "no," rewrite the statements so they are correct.
   Statements may vary. Example: Traits we inherit can affect how we look or how we function. Traits we get from experience can also affect how we look or how we function.
3. Look at this sheep. Write two traits the sheep inherited.
   Answers will vary.
   Write a trait the sheep got after it was born.
   a bite taken out of its ear

36 Life Science Science Lessons and Investigations • EMC 4313 • © Evan-Moor Corp.

Page 37

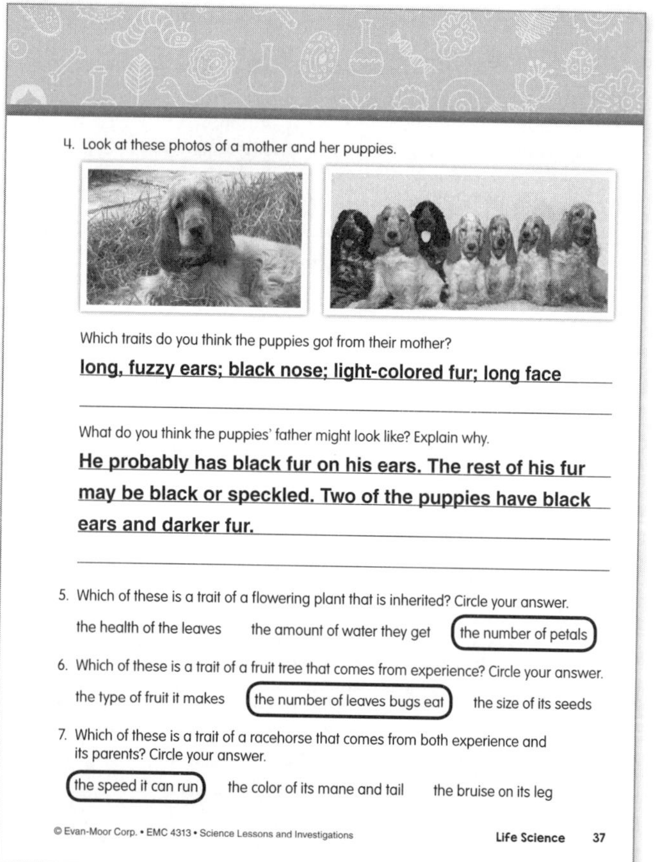

4. Look at these photos of a mother and her puppies.
   Which traits do you think the puppies got from their mother?
   long, fuzzy ears; black nose; light-colored fur; long face
   What do you think the puppies' father might look like? Explain why.
   He probably has black fur on his ears. The rest of his fur may be black or speckled. Two of the puppies have black ears and darker fur.
5. Which of these is a trait of a flowering plant that is inherited? Circle your answer.
   the health of the leaves the amount of water they get (the number of petals)
6. Which of these is a trait of a fruit tree that comes from experience? Circle your answer.
   the type of fruit it makes (the number of leaves bugs eat) the size of its seeds
7. Which of these is a trait of a racehorse that comes from both experience and its parents? Circle your answer.
   (the speed it can run) the color of its mane and tail the bruise on its leg

© Evan-Moor Corp. • EMC 4313 • Science Lessons and Investigations Life Science 37

Page 53

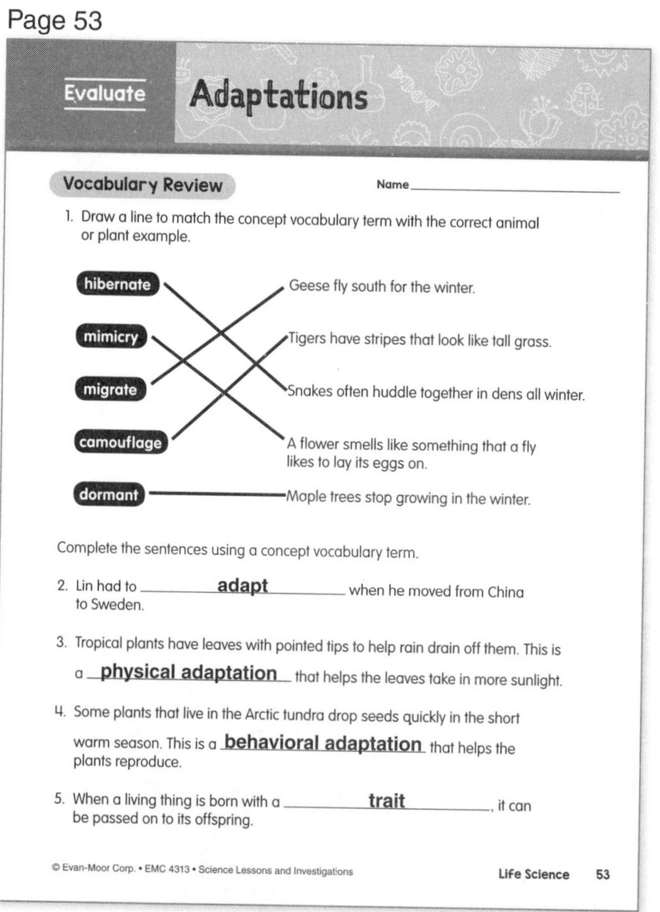

Evaluate — Adaptations

Vocabulary Review Name___________

1. Draw a line to match the concept vocabulary term with the correct animal or plant example.
   - hibernate — Geese fly south for the winter.
   - mimicry — Tigers have stripes that look like tall grass.
   - migrate — Snakes often huddle together in dens all winter.
   - camouflage — A flower smells like something that a fly likes to lay its eggs on.
   - dormant — Maple trees stop growing in the winter.

Complete the sentences using a concept vocabulary term.

2. Lin had to **adapt** when he moved from China to Sweden.
3. Tropical plants have leaves with pointed tips to help rain drain off them. This is a **physical adaptation** that helps the leaves take in more sunlight.
4. Some plants that live in the Arctic tundra drop seeds quickly in the short warm season. This is a **behavioral adaptation** that helps the plants reproduce.
5. When a living thing is born with a **trait**, it can be passed on to its offspring.

© Evan-Moor Corp. • EMC 4313 • Science Lessons and Investigations Life Science 53

Page 54

Adaptations

Evaluate

Concept Comprehension Name ____________

1. Imagine that a group of bugs live on large brown leaves. Some of the bugs are brown and some are green. Which bugs will probably survive? Explain.

The brown bugs will survive because they are camouflaged on the brown leaves. The green bugs will probably be eaten by the predators, who can easily see them.

2. Think about living things that hibernate and living things that go dormant. What do these adaptations have in common?

With both adaptations, the living thing is not active. It seems to sleep for a long time. It doesn't have to find or make food, eat, or reproduce.

How can you tell if a hedgehog is hibernating?

It looks like it is asleep. It might be in a warm, hidden place. The hedgehog feels colder than usual. It might not seem like it is breathing.

3. Many plants in the rainforest need sun to live and grow. However, some plants, such as orchids, do not grow tall. Instead, they grow on the tops of tall trees, not in the ground. Is this an example of a behavioral adaptation or a physical adaptation?

a behavioral adaptation

How does this adaptation help the plants that do not grow tall survive?

The plants need sunlight to survive, and the sunlight can reach them on top of tall trees.

54 Life Science Science Lessons and Investigations • EMC 4313 • © Evan-Moor Corp.

Page 55

4. Giraffes use their necks to reach leaves on tall trees. They also swing their necks when fighting for mates. Look at the pictures of two giraffes. Giraffe **A** has a short, thick neck. Giraffe **B** has a long, thin neck. Which one do you think is less likely to go hungry? Which one is more likely to find a mate? Explain your answers.

Giraffe B is less likely to go hungry. It has a long neck to reach the tree tops. Giraffe A is more likely to find a mate. Its thick neck is stronger.

5. Fill in the table to explain how each adaptation helps the animal or plant survive.

Adaptation	How it helps
A cactus plant stem can swell.	**A cactus stores more water in its stem to survive dry spells in the desert.**
Male peacocks have bright and colorful feathers.	**Bright feathers attract more mates. This helps peacocks reproduce.**
Bears hibernate in the winter.	**Bears sleep through bad weather when there is nothing to eat.**
An arctic fox has white fur.	**The fox is camouflaged in the snow. It helps the fox hide from predators and prey.**

© Evan-Moor Corp. • EMC 4313 • Science Lessons and Investigations Life Science 55

Page 70

Organisms in a Changing Environment

Evaluate

Vocabulary Review Name ____________

1. Look at the photo. Write three **physical characteristics** about the animal and the habitat.

animal	habitat
long antlers	**rocky mountain**
pointed ears	**tall trees**
skinny legs	**wide lake**

Answers will vary. Examples shown.

2. Draw an example for each term. Then explain your picture.

deforestation	native
Drawings will vary.	**Drawings will vary.**
In my picture, **Answers will vary.**	In my picture, **Answers will vary.**

3. Circle the example of an **organism**.

a chair (an insect) the wind

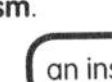

70 Life Science Science Lessons and Investigations • EMC 4313 • © Evan-Moor Corp.

Page 71

4. Complete the rhyme using terms from the Concept Vocabulary page.

A **habitat**, where a living thing lives,
Provides **resources** needed to grow and have kids.
If there is a **drought**, there is no rain for a time,
Or maybe it floods, or temperatures climb!
Ecosystems change in more ways than you think,
So living things change or become **extinct**.

5. A **haiku** is a short poem. It has only three lines. The first and last lines have 5 syllables. The second line has 7 syllables. This is an example of a haiku:

Resources

Natural from Earth
Others are made by people
These things are useful

Choose a concept vocabulary term and write a haiku about it. Then draw a picture.

concept vocabulary term: ____________

Answers will vary.

© Evan-Moor Corp. • EMC 4313 • Science Lessons and Investigations Life Science 71

Page 72

Evaluate

Organisms in a Changing Environment

Concept Comprehension Name

1. Which photo shows a change that caused a problem in the environment?

Explain the problem. **The paperbark trees took over and blocked the sunlight. Then native plants died. Then animals and bugs didn't have native plants to eat.**

2. Draw a picture in each box to show how brown tree snakes affected the numbers of birds and spiders.

Birds	Spiders
Answers and drawings may vary but should show one bird or a small number of birds.	**Answers and drawings may vary but should show a lot of spiders.**

Explain your drawings. **I drew one bird because the snakes ate a lot of the birds. Now there are not many left. Because the birds aren't eating the spiders, there are lots of spiders.**

Page 73

Scientists have been keeping track of where birds live in North America. They noticed that many birds are moving north. They made a graph to show how far north they now live. Look at the graph and answer questions 3 through 6.

How Far Bird Habitats Moved North

3. Which types of birds moved the farthest?

city birds

Name one kind of change these birds may have faced that made them move.

Answers will vary but should relate to city life.

4. The birds that were tracked changed their ______.

physical characteristics ~~behavior~~ (circled: behavior)

5. Why do you think all types of birds moved north instead of another direction?

The temperature is cooler the farther north you go, so maybe they were getting too hot where they used to be.

6. Look at the photo. Which type of bird from the graph do you think this is?

a wetland bird

Explain why you think so.

Its beak looks like it is adapted to scoop up food from water, like a deep spoon.

Page 86

Evaluate

Group Social Behavior

Vocabulary Review Name

1. Draw a picture that shows an example of each group of animals.

mob	waddle
drawing of meerkats	**drawing of penguins**
pod	**pack**
drawing of dolphins	**drawing of wolves**
colony	**school**
drawing of ants	**drawing of fish**

Page 87

2. Which sentence describes a **group behavior**?

○ In the fall, brown bears eat up to 90 pounds of food a day to prepare to hibernate.

● Lions hunt together to catch prey that are often bigger than they are.

○ A leopard hides in tall grass before it lunges at its prey.

3. Which photo shows people in a **huddle**?

●

○

4. Complete the paragraph using concept vocabulary terms.

Jalen was nervous as he waited outside the ballpark. Today he was going to try out for Little League. He looked at the other players who were trying out. Many were taller and stronger-looking. This would give them an **advantage**. But there was no turning back now. The coach opened the door and began to **herd** all the athletes into the stands. It was time to start the tryouts. Jalen tried not to think about how his skinny arms and short legs put him at a **disadvantage**. Jalen took a deep breath as he got ready to fight for a spot on a team.

Page 88

Evaluate Group Social Behavior

Concept Comprehension Name

1. Fill in the table with three reasons animals live in groups. Then give an example of each.

Reason animals live in groups	Example
to gather food	**Wolves hunt together to eat bigger prey.**
for safety and protection	**A meerkat watches for predators while others do work.**
to work together	**Ants reach safety in a flood.**

2. Humans live in groups, too. Give two examples of how humans work together to survive.

Parents help children when they are sick or hurt.

Farmers grow large amounts of food for many people.

3. Animal groups can vary in size. Think about one need that groups have. Compare how life would be for a small group and a large group.

Answers will vary. Example shown.

A small group doesn't need as much food. A large group has more members to gather or hunt for, but it also has more hunters.

Page 89

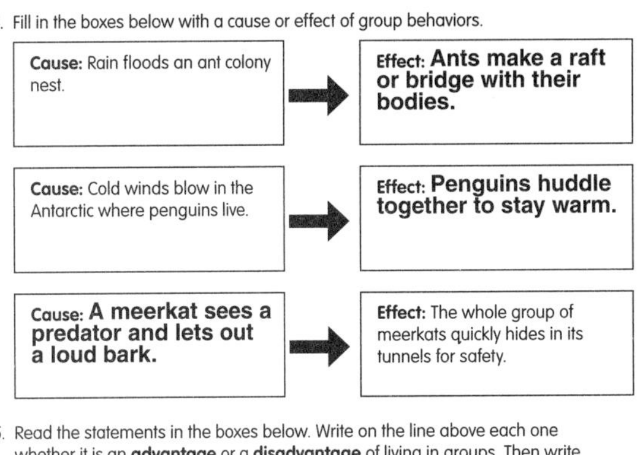

4. Fill in the boxes below with a cause or effect of group behaviors.

Cause		Effect
Cause: Rain floods an ant colony nest.	→	**Effect: Ants make a raft or bridge with their bodies.**
Cause: Cold winds blow in the Antarctic where penguins live.	→	**Effect: Penguins huddle together to stay warm.**
Cause: A meerkat sees a predator and lets out a loud bark.	→	**Effect:** The whole group of meerkats quickly hides in its tunnels for safety.

5. Read the statements in the boxes below. Write on the line above each one whether it is an **advantage** or a **disadvantage** of living in groups. Then write another advantage and disadvantage of living in groups in the bottom boxes.

disadvantage	**advantage**
Disease spreads faster in groups.	There are more members to help take care of the young.
Predators can easily spot large groups.	**It is easier to stay warm in groups.**

Answers will vary. Example shown.

Page 102

Evaluate Fossils of Ancestors

Vocabulary Review Name

Orders may vary.

1. Describe four types of fossils. Then write each letter next to its photo.

a. **bone or other hard body part**

b. **mold with spaces where the animal rotted away**

c. **cast with minerals making the animal's or plant's shape**

d. **trace fossil that shows a mark the animal left**

b

a

d

c

Page 103

2. Look at the diagram. Label the **fossil** and the **sediment**.

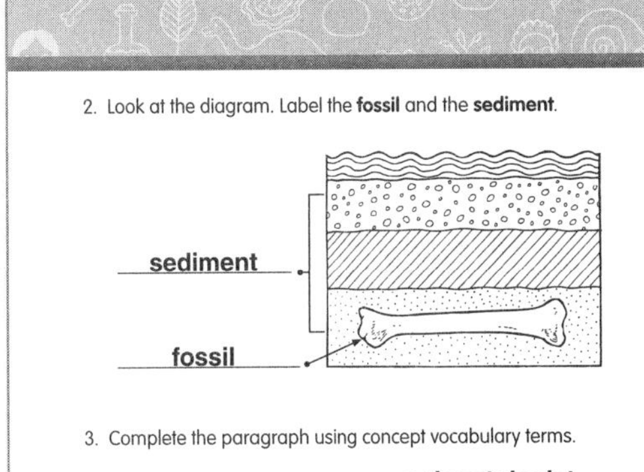

3. Complete the paragraph using concept vocabulary terms.

Robert hadn't planned to be a **paleontologist**. He grew up in northern Alaska. It's so cold there that the ground stays frozen all year long. But the rivers and streams melt in the short summer. One summer, Robert was looking for gold in a riverbed. Out of the corner of his eye, he saw something odd. He looked over at the **sedimentary rock**. In one of the layers, he spotted a strange-looking bone. He ran home and brought his mother back. Together, they carefully **excavated** the bone. It turned out to be a long mammoth tusk! Unfortunately, the rest of the mammoth's body had **decayed**. But Robert's first piece of **evidence** proved that he and mammoths, which are **extinct**, had wandered the same land.

Page 104

Evaluate Fossils of Ancestors

Concept Comprehension Name

1. What is the difference between a dead plant and an extinct plant?
   There may be other living plants just like the dead plant somewhere else. If a plant is extinct, there are no more alive like it anywhere on Earth; the whole
2. What are two liquids in which you might find fossils containing body parts of animals?
   amber asphalt
3. Write three examples of information that fossils can tell us about extinct animals.
   Answers may vary but may include body structure and size, what it ate, how it walked, if it traveled in groups.

   What can an amber fossil tell scientists that a trace fossil cannot tell them?
   Answers may vary. Example shown. An amber fossil shows exactly how the animal's body looked. A trace fossil can tell only about its feet, its size, and how it walked.
4. Paleontologists have found dinosaur skulls with sharp teeth and others with flat teeth. What do you think this difference could tell scientists?
   It could tell them what they ate or that they ate different things.

104 Life Science Science Lessons and Investigations • EMC 4313 • © Evan-Moor Corp.

Page 105

5. Write **true** or **false**.
   a. Fossils form quickly and are very common. false
   b. Sand and soil are two kinds of sediment. true
   c. A dead plant will turn into a fossil within ten years. false
   d. Minerals take the place of bones in cast fossils. true
   e. Dinosaurs went extinct about 65 million years ago. true
   f. Shells, teeth, and bones decay in sediment. false
   g. Humans and dinosaurs lived during the same time. false
   h. Minerals are nonliving things. true

Use the diagram to help you answer questions 6 and 7.

6. Are the oldest fossils likely to be in the top layer, middle layer, or bottom layer? Explain why.
   They're probably in the bottom layer because as time passes, fossils usually get covered up more and more.

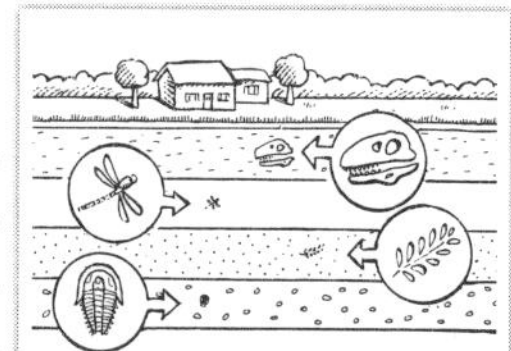

7. If paleontologists found a fossil in the middle layer that was 2 million years old, would they think that Earth was more or less than 2 million years old? Why?
   They would think Earth was more than 2 million years old. Any fossils below the middle layer would be older, so Earth must be older, too.

© Evan-Moor Corp. • EMC 4313 • Science Lessons and Investigations Life Science 105

Page 118

Evaluate Weather

Vocabulary Review Name

Complete the sentences using concept vocabulary terms.

1. When a cloud collects enough water V A P O [R], it rains.
2. Most people like sunny W [E] A T H E R, but I like it foggy.
3. My aunt used a T H E R M O M E T E R to check my cousin's temperature when he was sick.
4. The [A] T M O S P H E R E protects our planet in many ways.
5. Jamila read the R A I N G A [U] G E after last night's storm.
6. I refill my dog's water bowl daily because of E V A P O R A T I O [N].
7. I wonder how many times a drop of water goes through the W A T E R C Y C [L] E in a year.
8. My coat keeps me dry in all kinds of P R E C I P I T [A] T I O N.
9. The way the A N E [M] O M E T E R is spinning around, I should go fly a kite!
10. Milo wiped the C O N D E N S A T I O N off the outside of the cold soda can.
11. The M E T E O R O [L] O G I S T checks weather instruments several times a day.
12. The W I N D V A N E usually points to the east in the morning.

Now arrange all of the letters in boxes above to answer the riddle.

What goes up when rain comes down?

A N U M b R E L L A

118 Earth Science Science Lessons and Investigations • EMC 4313 • © Evan-Moor Corp.

Page 119

Evaluate Weather

Concept Comprehension Name

1. True or false: Weather happens in the atmosphere. true
2. How does water get into the atmosphere?
   It evaporates, changing from water to gas.

   How do clouds and rain form?
   Water evaporates and then condenses and forms clouds. When the water droplets are heavy enough, they fall as rain.
3. Some students asked questions about the weather. Choose the best tool to answer each question.

   thermometer anemometer wind vane rain gauge

   a. Which way is the wind blowing? wind vane
   b. How hot is it outside? thermometer
   c. How fast is the wind blowing? anemometer
   d. How much rain fell yesterday? rain gauge
4. Circle the underlined part that answers the question.
   a. Does temperature tell (how warm) or how wet something is?
   b. Is snow atmosphere or (precipitation)?
   c. Does an anemometer measure (wind speed) or direction?
   d. Does a meteorologist (predict the weather) or study space?
   e. Is water vapor in the ocean or in the (atmosphere)?

© Evan-Moor Corp. • EMC 4313 • Science Lessons and Investigations Earth Science 119

Page 120

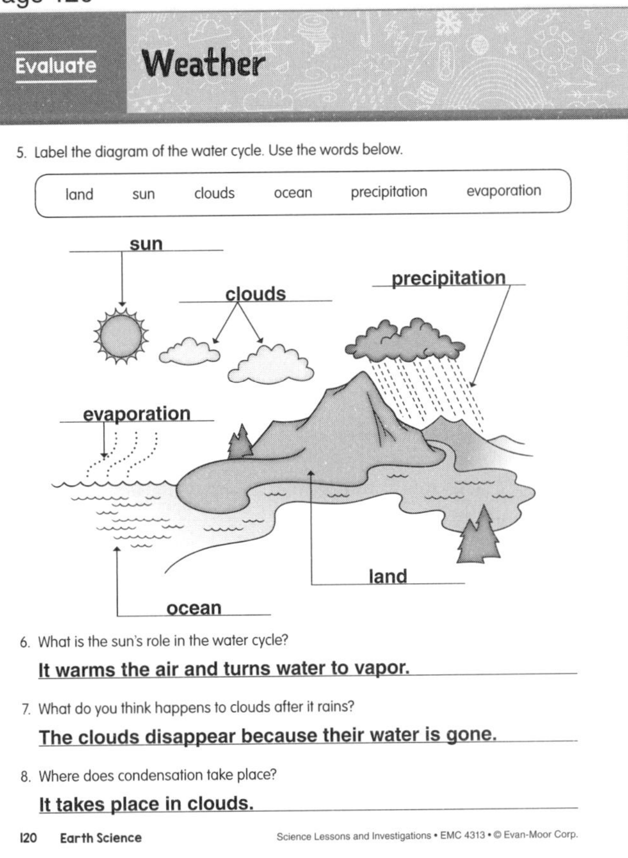

Evaluate **Weather**

5. Label the diagram of the water cycle. Use the words below.

land sun clouds ocean precipitation evaporation

6. What is the sun's role in the water cycle?
It warms the air and turns water to vapor.

7. What do you think happens to clouds after it rains?
The clouds disappear because their water is gone.

8. Where does condensation take place?
It takes place in clouds.

120 Earth Science Science Lessons and Investigations • EMC 4313 • © Evan-Moor Corp.

Page 121

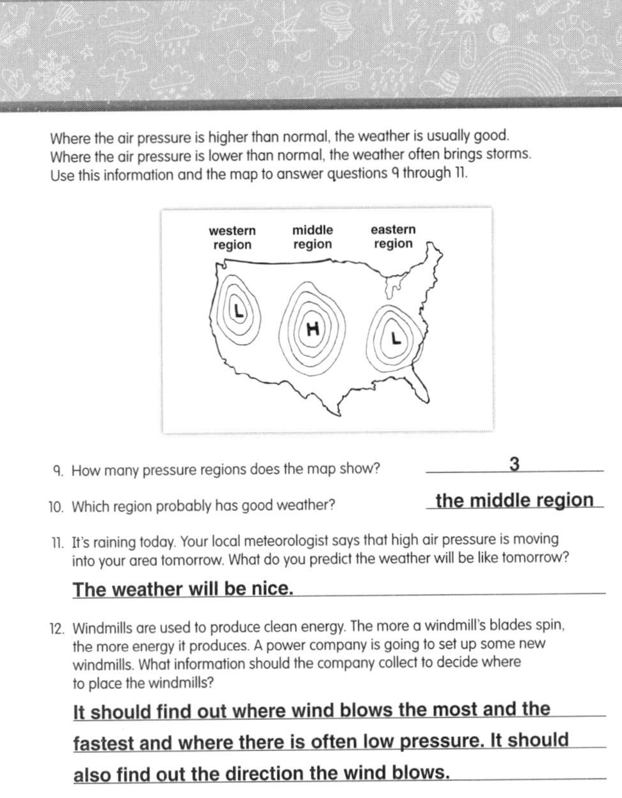

Where the air pressure is higher than normal, the weather is usually good. Where the air pressure is lower than normal, the weather often brings storms. Use this information and the map to answer questions 9 through 11.

9. How many pressure regions does the map show? **3**

10. Which region probably has good weather? **the middle region**

11. It's raining today. Your local meteorologist says that high air pressure is moving into your area tomorrow. What do you predict the weather will be like tomorrow?
The weather will be nice.

12. Windmills are used to produce clean energy. The more a windmill's blades spin, the more energy it produces. A power company is going to set up some new windmills. What information should the company collect to decide where to place the windmills?
It should find out where wind blows the most and the fastest and where there is often low pressure. It should also find out the direction the wind blows.

© Evan-Moor Corp. • EMC 4313 • Science Lessons and Investigations Earth Science 121

Page 136

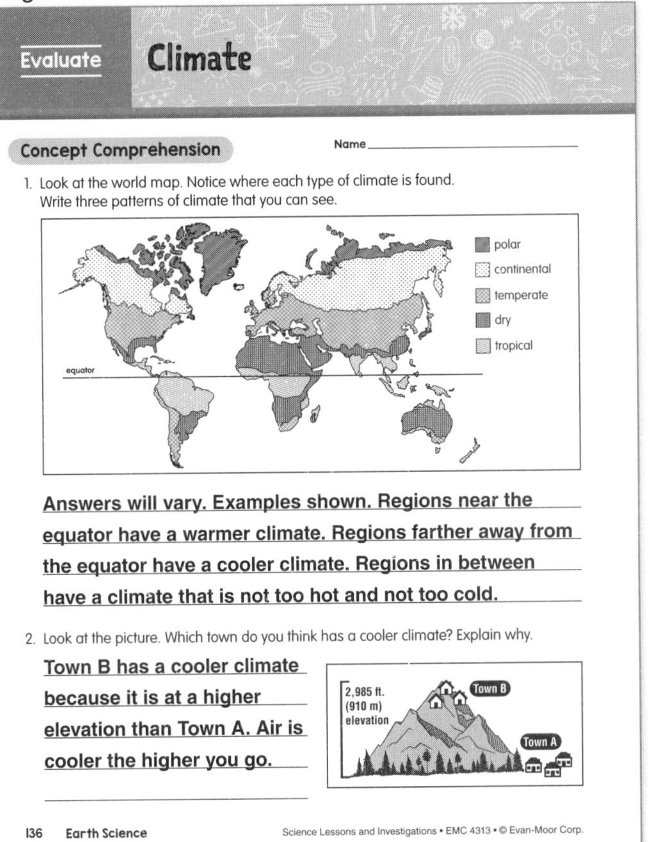

Evaluate **Climate**

Concept Comprehension Name ____________

1. Look at the world map. Notice where each type of climate is found. Write three patterns of climate that you can see.

Answers will vary. Examples shown. Regions near the equator have a warmer climate. Regions farther away from the equator have a cooler climate. Regions in between have a climate that is not too hot and not too cold.

2. Look at the picture. Which town do you think has a cooler climate? Explain why.

Town B has a cooler climate because it is at a higher elevation than Town A. Air is cooler the higher you go.

136 Earth Science Science Lessons and Investigations • EMC 4313 • © Evan-Moor Corp.

Page 137

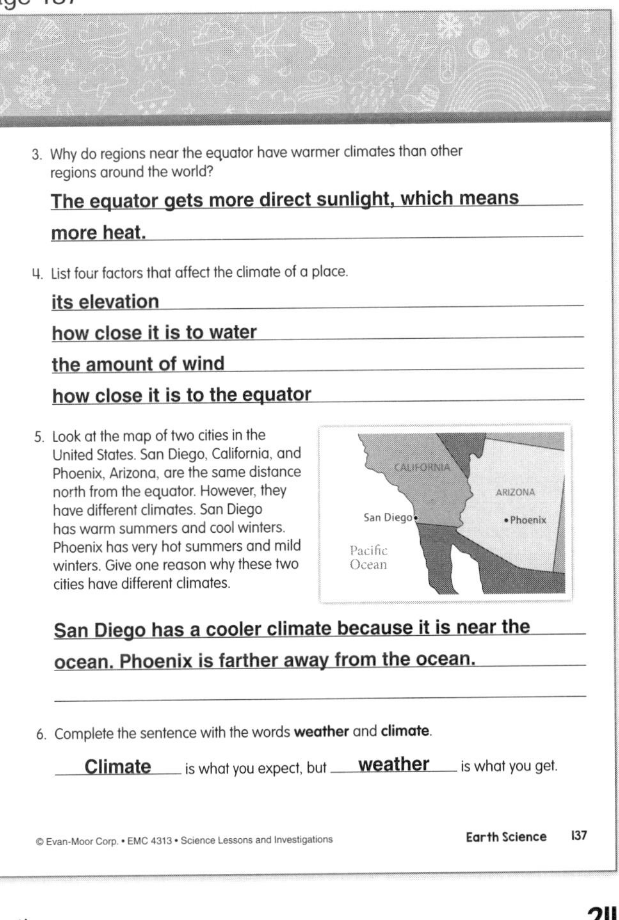

3. Why do regions near the equator have warmer climates than other regions around the world?
The equator gets more direct sunlight, which means more heat.

4. List four factors that affect the climate of a place.
its elevation
how close it is to water
the amount of wind
how close it is to the equator

5. Look at the map of two cities in the United States. San Diego, California, and Phoenix, Arizona, are the same distance north from the equator. However, they have different climates. San Diego has warm summers and cool winters. Phoenix has very hot summers and mild winters. Give one reason why these two cities have different climates.

San Diego has a cooler climate because it is near the ocean. Phoenix is farther away from the ocean.

6. Complete the sentence with the words **weather** and **climate**.
Climate is what you expect, but **weather** is what you get.

© Evan-Moor Corp. • EMC 4313 • Science Lessons and Investigations Earth Science 137

Page 150

Evaluate

Natural Processes and Hazards

Vocabulary Review

Name ______________

Complete the paragraphs using concept vocabulary terms.

1. The Nile River in Africa is the longest river in the world. In ancient times in Egypt, water flowed over the **banks** of the Nile River every year, causing a **flood**. Today, there is a huge **dam** on the Nile at Aswan, Egypt. It was built in 1970. It controls extra water in the rainy season and stores it to be used later.

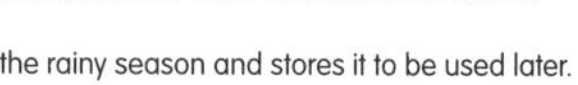

2. The country of Chile is located on the coast of the Pacific Ocean. There is a crack underneath the sea where two pieces of Earth's **crust** meet. In 2010, there was a strong **earthquake** in Chile. Buildings were destroyed. The shaking caused giant waves in the ocean, which came onshore. The homes of many people were washed away.

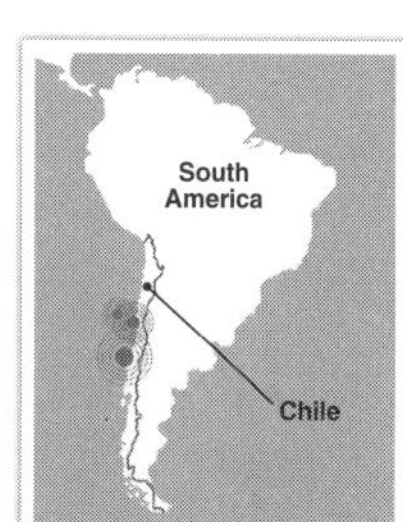

Page 151

Evaluate

Natural Processes and Hazards

3. Nearly 150 years ago in 1883, the Krakatoa **volcano** erupted in the country of Indonesia. Enormous amounts of **magma** rose from the **mantle**. Some of the **lava** that came out of Krakatoa's **vent** flowed into the sea and boiled the water into steam. The eruption was so huge that it destroyed most of the island it was on. The sound could be heard in Australia, more than 2,000 miles (3,600 kilometers) away!

Indonesia
Verlaten Island
Lang Island
destroyed land
Krakatoa Island

Page 152

Evaluate

Natural Processes and Hazards

Concept Comprehension

Name ______________

1. Label the parts of the volcano using the words **crust**, **lava**, and **magma**.
   a. **magma**
   b. **crust**
   c. **lava**

2. Where does magma comes from?
   a. the sky
   b. the crust
   c. the ocean
   (d.) the mantle

3. What causes earthquakes?
   a. crust breaking into small pieces
   b. ice sliding on top of the crust
   (c.) pieces of crust hitting or scraping each other
   d. pieces of crust coming up from the mantle

4. Which of these is true about floods?
   a. Floods are hard to predict.
   (b.) Floods have several causes.
   c. Floods happen mostly on the coasts.
   d. Floods are not as dangerous as other hazards.

Page 153

5. People should be prepared before a natural disaster happens because they may not have electricity and may not be able to buy food or water. What other things would you need to have? Why would you need them?

   Answers will vary. Example: I want a blanket in case it gets cold. I want my cellphone to see if my friends are okay. I want some clothes to change into.

6. Write one way that floods are helpful and one way they are harmful.

   Helpful: **They bring new soil to an area.**

   Harmful: **They cause damage and destroy crops.**

7. How do dams help control flooding?

   Dams hold back a lot of water. They have gates to let it out or keep it in. They don't let the water flow freely.

8. Write three ways to stay safe in a flood.

   Travel to higher ground or to a higher floor.
   Don't go through a flooded area.
   Leave the area.

9. Why do you think scientists are trying to find ways to predict natural hazards?

   Answers will vary. Example: If they can figure out when they are going to happen, they can warn everyone in the area. That way, people can get to safety in time.

Page 167

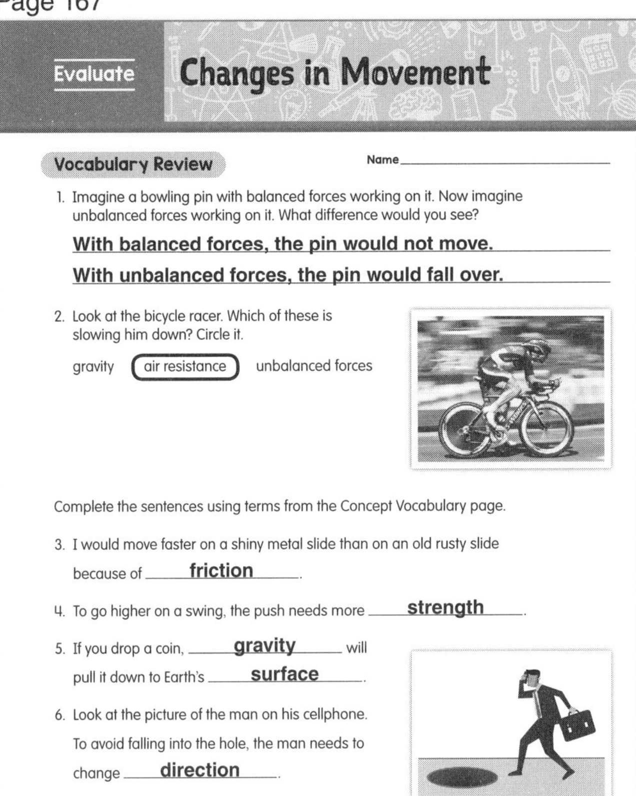

Evaluate

Changes in Movement

Vocabulary Review

Name ____________________

1. Imagine a bowling pin with balanced forces working on it. Now imagine unbalanced forces working on it. What difference would you see?

   With balanced forces, the pin would not move.

   With unbalanced forces, the pin would fall over.

2. Look at the bicycle racer. Which of these is slowing him down? Circle it.

   gravity (air resistance) unbalanced forces

Complete the sentences using terms from the Concept Vocabulary page.

3. I would move faster on a shiny metal slide than on an old rusty slide because of **friction**.
4. To go higher on a swing, the push needs more **strength**.
5. If you drop a coin, **gravity** will pull it down to Earth's **surface**.
6. Look at the picture of the man on his cellphone. To avoid falling into the hole, the man needs to change **direction**.

© Evan-Moor Corp. • EMC 4313 • Science Lessons and Investigations Physical Science 167

Page 168

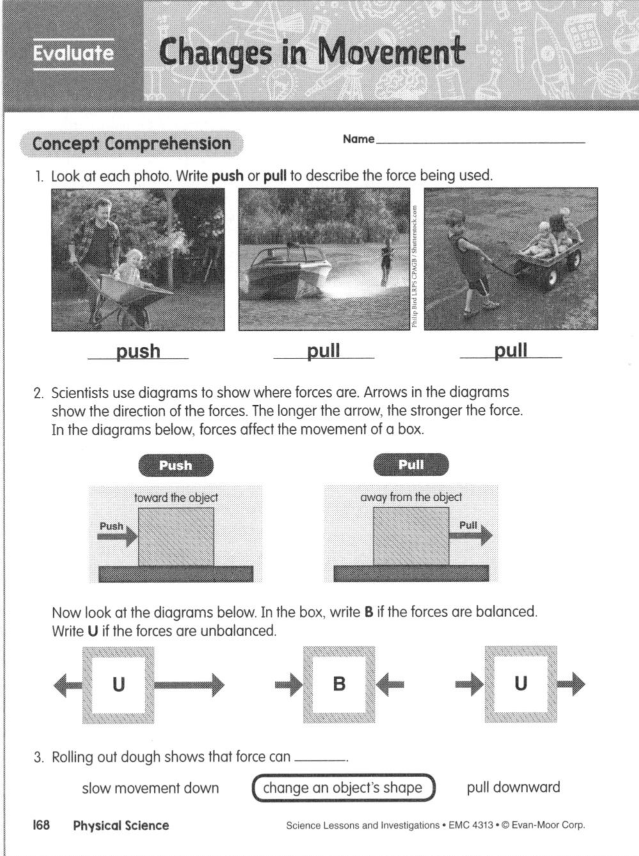

Evaluate

Changes in Movement

Concept Comprehension

Name ____________________

1. Look at each photo. Write **push** or **pull** to describe the force being used.

   push **pull** **pull**

2. Scientists use diagrams to show where forces are. Arrows in the diagrams show the direction of the forces. The longer the arrow, the stronger the force. In the diagrams below, forces affect the movement of a box.

   Now look at the diagrams below. In the box, write **B** if the forces are balanced. Write **U** if the forces are unbalanced.

   U **B** **U**

3. Rolling out dough shows that force can ______.

   slow movement down (change an object's shape) pull downward

168 Physical Science Science Lessons and Investigations • EMC 4313 • © Evan-Moor Corp.

Page 169

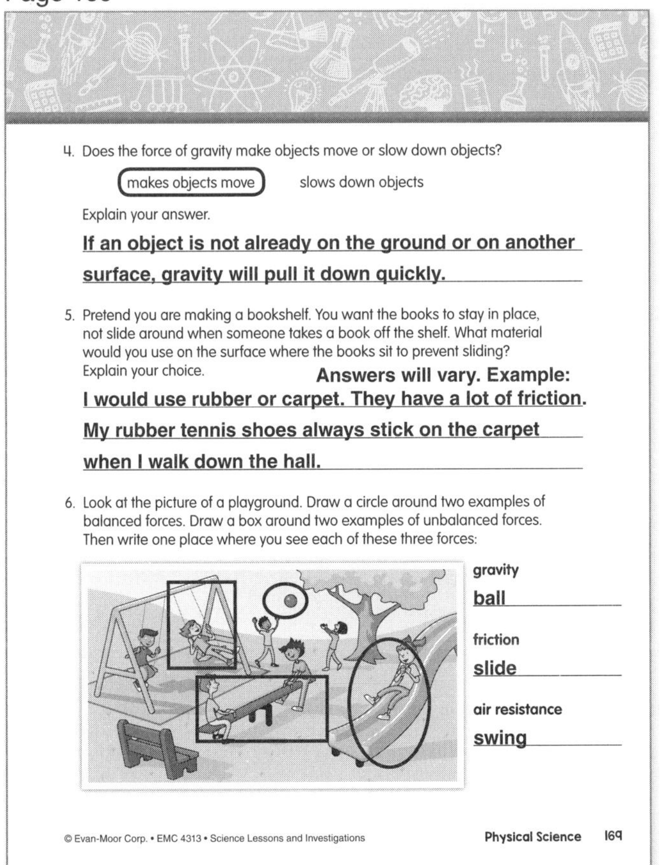

4. Does the force of gravity make objects move or slow down objects?

   (makes objects move) slows down objects

   Explain your answer.

   If an object is not already on the ground or on another surface, gravity will pull it down quickly.

5. Pretend you are making a bookshelf. You want the books to stay in place, not slide around when someone takes a book off the shelf. What material would you use on the surface where the books sit to prevent sliding? Explain your choice. **Answers will vary. Example:**

   I would use rubber or carpet. They have a lot of friction. My rubber tennis shoes always stick on the carpet when I walk down the hall.

6. Look at the picture of a playground. Draw a circle around two examples of balanced forces. Draw a box around two examples of unbalanced forces. Then write one place where you see each of these three forces:

   gravity **ball**

   friction **slide**

   air resistance **swing**

© Evan-Moor Corp. • EMC 4313 • Science Lessons and Investigations Physical Science 169

Page 182

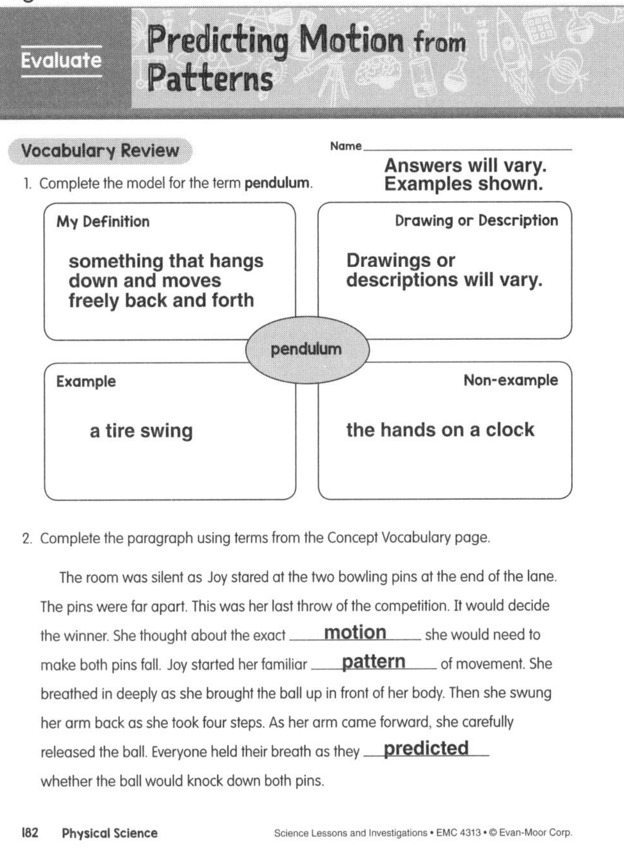

Evaluate

Predicting Motion from Patterns

Vocabulary Review

Name ____________________

Answers will vary. Examples shown.

1. Complete the model for the term **pendulum**.

My Definition	Drawing or Description
something that hangs down and moves freely back and forth	**Drawings or descriptions will vary.**
Example	**Non-example**
a tire swing	**the hands on a clock**

pendulum

2. Complete the paragraph using terms from the Concept Vocabulary page.

   The room was silent as Joy stared at the two bowling pins at the end of the lane. The pins were far apart. This was her last throw of the competition. It would decide the winner. She thought about the exact **motion** she would need to make both pins fall. Joy started her familiar **pattern** of movement. She breathed in deeply as she brought the ball up in front of her body. Then she swung her arm back as she took four steps. As her arm came forward, she carefully released the ball. Everyone held their breath as they **predicted** whether the ball would knock down both pins.

182 Physical Science Science Lessons and Investigations • EMC 4313 • © Evan-Moor Corp.

Page 183

Evaluate

Predicting Motion from Patterns

3. Draw an animal or an object moving in each pattern. **Answers will vary. Examples shown.**

circular	spiral
drawing of stirring a liquid	**drawing of a spiral staircase**
serpentine	**zigzag**
drawing of fish swimming	**drawing of slalom skiing**

4. How are the circular and spiral movements similar and different?

similar: **They go around.**

different: **Circular movement goes around the center. Spiral movement moves away from the center.**

5. How are the serpentine and zigzag movements similar and different?

similar: **They go side to side but also forward.**

different: **Serpentine movement is curvy. Zigzag movement has straight lines.**

Page 184

Evaluate

Predicting Motion from Patterns

Answers will vary. Examples shown.

Concept Comprehension Name________

1. Look at the photo of a tennis player about to hit a ball. Predict the player's motion and the ball's motion. Describe both.

Her arm will swing forward a little.
The ball will change direction.
The ball will go forward fast.
The player will stop moving forward.

2. You come to a stoplight walking home from school. You press a button to stop the cars so you can cross the street safely. The light changes and you see the "walk" symbol. The symbol blinks as it counts down from 20. What pattern do you see? How will it help you cross safely?

I see how fast the numbers change each time it blinks. I can see how far I have left to cross and how much time I have left. I can walk faster if time is running out.

3. Write the name of a team sport that uses a pattern of motion. **baseball**

Describe one pattern's direction and speed. **The ball is pitched forward and it moves fast. If the batter doesn't hit it, the ball curves down and the catcher stops it.**

How do players use this pattern to help them play the game? **The batter looks for the exact height and aims the bat.**

Page 185

Evaluate

Predicting Motion from Patterns

4. When Mr. Ogren's students came back from lunch, Sam noticed that Sally Snail, the class pet, had crawled out of her box. Think about a snail's pattern of movement. Where should Sam start looking for Sally?

Snails crawl slowly, so Sam should look all around close to the box.

5. The weather forecast calls for strong winds to blow toward the west tonight. Here is Kemi's yard. Predict how it will look when the winds are blowing. Draw how the yard will look after the winds blow.

Before

After

Drawing shows leaves scattered westward, cans, and rake on ground facing west

6. Ravi just jumped off the swing as it swung forward. Draw the next four movements of the empty swing.

Swing is back, forward, back, and forward, a little closer to center each time.

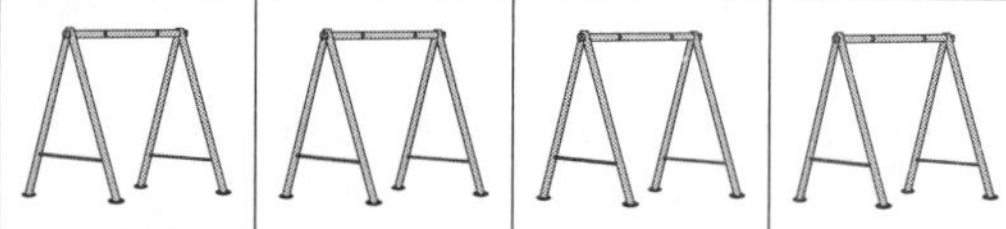

Page 199

Evaluate

Magnetic Forces

Vocabulary Review Name________

Answers will vary. Examples shown:

1. Complete the model for the term **attract**.

My Definition	Drawing or Description
to make something come closer	**It's a force that can make certain things move just by being near them.**
Example	**Non-example**
A magnet pulls other magnets toward it.	**a piece of metal that doesn't move toward a magnet**

attract

Complete the sentences using terms from the Concept Vocabulary page.

2. When the entry **pole** of one magnet is near the entry **pole** of another magnet, the magnets will **repel** one another.
3. A magnet pulls paper clips toward it because they have **iron** in them.
4. A magnet does not need to touch an object to pull it. As long as the object is in the **magnetic field** of a magnet, the magnet can pull the object.
5. Some people put **magnetic** letters on their refrigerators to spell words.
6. You can't see the force of **magnetism**, but you can see it pull and push objects.

Page 200

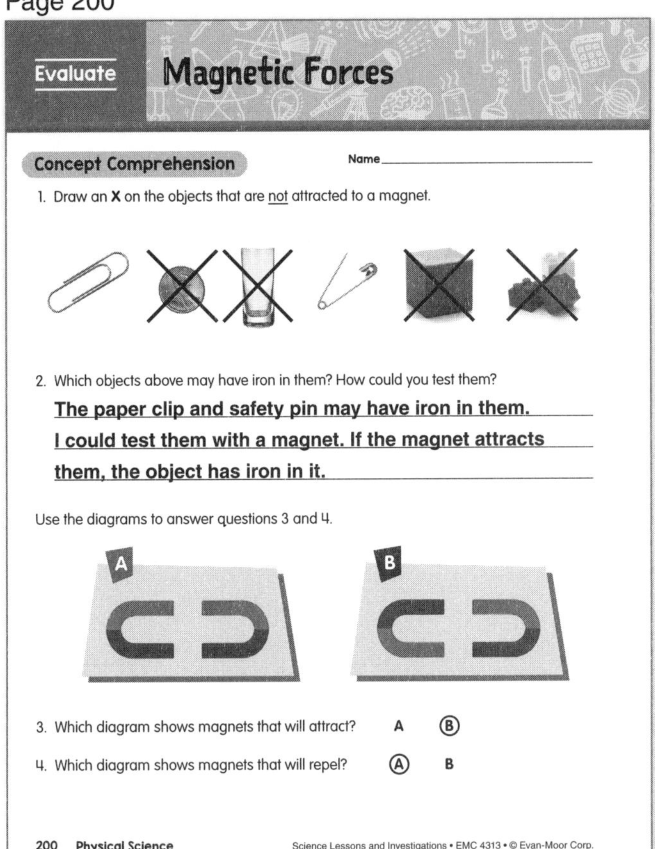

Evaluate

Magnetic Forces

Concept Comprehension

Name

1. Draw an **X** on the objects that are not attracted to a magnet.

2. Which objects above may have iron in them? How could you test them?

The paper clip and safety pin may have iron in them. I could test them with a magnet. If the magnet attracts them, the object has iron in it.

Use the diagrams to answer questions 3 and 4.

3. Which diagram shows magnets that will attract? A Ⓑ

4. Which diagram shows magnets that will repel? Ⓐ B

200 Physical Science

Science Lessons and Investigations • EMC 4313 • © Evan-Moor Corp.

Page 201

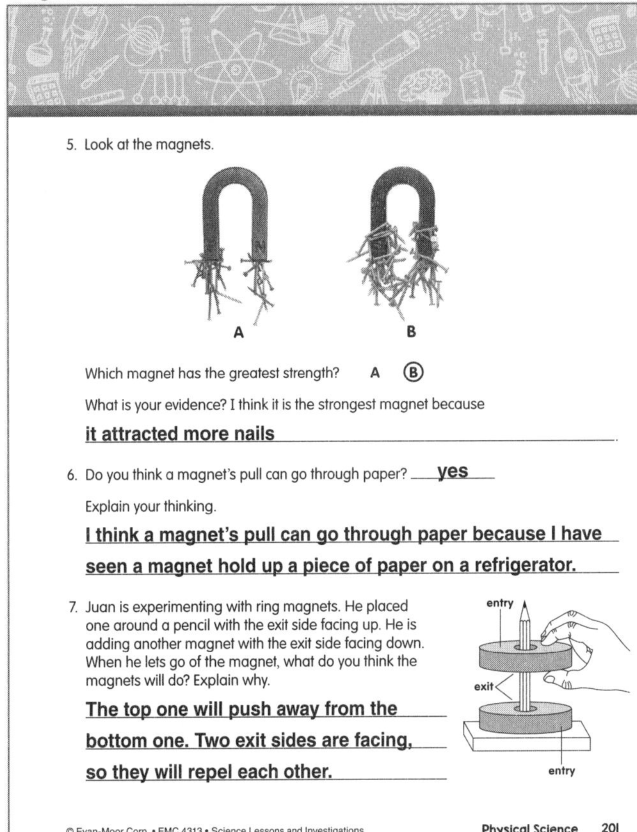

5. Look at the magnets.

Which magnet has the greatest strength? A Ⓑ

What is your evidence? I think it is the strongest magnet because **it attracted more nails**.

6. Do you think a magnet's pull can go through paper? **yes**

Explain your thinking.

I think a magnet's pull can go through paper because I have seen a magnet hold up a piece of paper on a refrigerator.

7. Juan is experimenting with ring magnets. He placed one around a pencil with the exit side facing up. He is adding another magnet with the exit side facing down. When he lets go of the magnet, what do you think the magnets will do? Explain why.

The top one will push away from the bottom one. Two exit sides are facing, so they will repel each other.

© Evan-Moor Corp. • EMC 4313 • Science Lessons and Investigations

Physical Science 201

Daily Science

GRADE 3

SAMPLER

Living things have adaptations that help them survive in their environment.

Week 3

Why does a cactus have needles?

This week, students learn about a cactus's adaptations. In order to survive in a desert environment, cacti have many adaptations. Instead of broad, flat leaves, cacti have needles, or spines. Spines create shade for the cactus, preventing water loss from sun exposure. They help the plant collect water from fog and dew, directing it to drip on the long, shallow roots below. The spines also deter animals that are seeking water, and provide shelter for some birds, such as mourning doves, who nest in cacti for protection.

Day One

Vocabulary: *evaporate*

Activate prior knowledge by asking students to list features of a desert. (dry, hot, sunny, sandy, few plants and animals, etc.) Distribute page 21 and introduce the vocabulary word. Then have volunteers read the introduction aloud. Point out the picture of the cactus and ask students to describe what they see. (spines, ridges or folds in the skin, flowers, etc.) Then have students complete the activities. Review the answers together.

Day Two

Vocabulary: *spine*

Distribute page 22 and introduce the vocabulary word, pointing out the difference in meaning from the one students are probably familiar with. (backbone) Discuss the qualities of a cactus's spines. (sharp, thin, hard, etc.) Then ask students to think what the spines might be good for. (protection) Have volunteers read the introduction aloud and then have students complete the activities. Review the answers together.

Day Three

Materials: pictures of a cactus and a porcupine (optional)

Distribute page 23. Have volunteers read the introduction aloud. Then point out the picture of the cholla on the page and brainstorm with students other plants that have similar adaptations. (Roses have thorns; bark protects trees; burrs stick to socks; etc.) Have students complete the activities. For activity B, give students background information about porcupines, if needed. Then review the answers together.

Day Four

Vocabulary: *folds*

Distribute page 24 and introduce the vocabulary word. Then have volunteers read the introduction aloud. You may also want to read aloud the adaptations and conditions listed in activity A. Then have students complete the activities. Review the answers together.

Day Five

Tell students they will review everything they have learned about a cactus's adaptations. Have students complete page 25. Then go over the answers together.

Name ______________________________

Day 1

Weekly Question

Why does a cactus have needles?

It is difficult for living things to survive in deserts because most deserts are dry and hot. It may not rain for months. When it does rain, the hot, dry weather makes the water quickly **evaporate**. Without clouds, there is little shade from the sun. A desert plant, such as a cactus, must adapt to the harsh desert conditions in order to stay alive and grow.

Vocabulary

evaporate
to change from a liquid to a gas

A. What are two things that make life in the desert difficult?

1. ______________________________

2. ______________________________

B. Read each question. Check the box next to the correct answer.

1. Based on what you know about the desert, which of these animals could survive in the desert?

- ❒ a kangaroo rat that needs little water
- ❒ a white-tailed deer that eats pine tree needles
- ❒ a polar bear with thick fur to protect it from the cold

2. Which one would cause water in a cup to evaporate faster?

- ❒ leaving it by the window on a cool, cloudy day
- ❒ leaving it by the window on a warm, sunny day

Name ________________________________

Day 2

Weekly Question

Why does a cactus have needles?

The needles on a cactus, called **spines**, are actually a kind of leaf. The spine is an adaptation of a regular leaf to help the cactus survive in the desert. Just as there are different kinds of leaves, there are different kinds of cactus spines. Some help the cactus collect rain. These long spines direct water to the cactus's roots.

Other kinds of spines grow thickly over the cactus. They protect it from the sun and help keep the cactus from drying out. Water is less likely to evaporate if the sun is not shining directly on the cactus's skin.

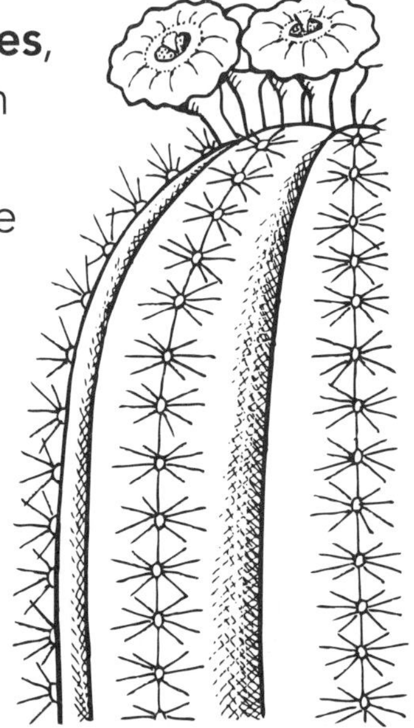

saguaro cactus

Vocabulary

spine
a stiff, sharp needle of a cactus

A. Check the box next to the word that completes each sentence.

1. Spines are an adaptation of _____.

❒ leaves ❒ roots ❒ flowers

2. Some spines on a cactus help collect _____.

❒ sunlight ❒ water ❒ sand

3. Some kinds of spines protect the cactus from _____.

❒ rain ❒ cold ❒ sunlight

B. Predict what would probably happen to the leaves of a regular plant in the desert.

____

Name ______________________________

Day 3

Weekly Question

Why does a cactus have needles?

Spines do more than help a cactus survive in desert conditions. They protect the cactus from animals looking for a juicy meal. The spines break off easily and will stick in an animal's mouth if it tries to eat the cactus.

Some spines also help the cactus reproduce. For example, the jumping cholla (CHOY-ah) breaks apart easily when an animal brushes against it. The spines make the broken-off piece stick to the passing animal. When the cactus piece finally drops off, it grows roots and becomes a new plant!

jumping cholla

A. Explain how animals help the jumping cholla reproduce.

____

____

B. A porcupine is an animal that has sharp needles, called quills, on its body. How do you think a porcupine's quills might be similar to a cactus's spines?

____

C. Write **true** or **false**.

1. A cactus's spines are sharp like needles. ____________

2. A cactus uses its spines to attract animals. ____________

Name ____

Weekly Question

Why does a cactus have needles?

Spines aren't the only adaptations a cactus has for surviving in the desert. Some cacti have **folds** that can swell and store hundreds of gallons of water. Their roots are shallow and spread far from the plant. The roots are ready to drink up even the smallest amount of rain. The thick, waxy skin of the cactus keeps the water inside from evaporating.

Vocabulary

folds
bends or ridges that allow something to get bigger

A. Draw a line to match how each adaptation helps the cactus survive in the desert.

Adaptation			Desert Condition
folds that swell and store water	•	•	heat that causes water to quickly evaporate after it lands
shallow roots that absorb rain quickly	•	•	a lot of sunlight without shade
thick skin that protects the cactus	•	•	long periods of time without rain

B. Look at the diagram.
Label the **folds**, **roots**, and **flower**.

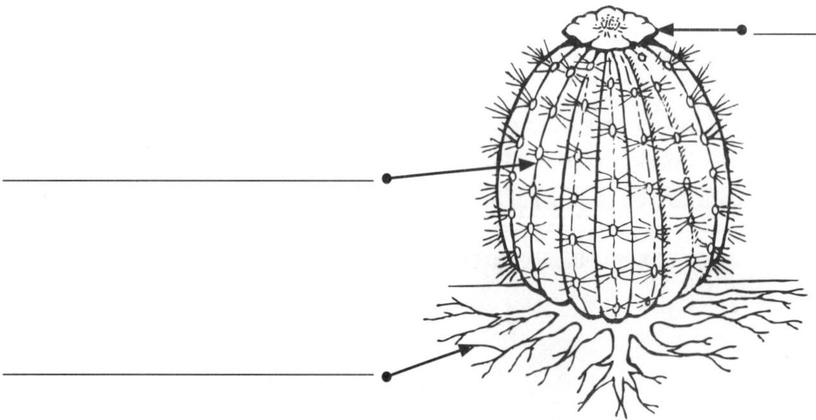

Name ____________________________________

Day 5

Weekly Question

Why does a cactus have needles?

A. Describe two jobs that a cactus's spines can do to help the cactus survive in the desert.

1. ____________________________________

2. ____________________________________

B. Use the words in the box to complete the paragraph.

evaporate	**survive**	**folds**	**spines**

A cactus is adapted to ______________ in a hot, dry desert. It stores up water and uses the water slowly. The thick, waxy skin of the cactus helps make sure that the water doesn't ______________. Sharp ______________ protect the plant. They also help it collect water. The ______________ of the cactus allow it to store as much water as possible.

C. Which analogy is correct? Check the box next to it.

- ❒ **Spines** are to **cactus** as **flowers** are to **plant.**
- ❒ **Spines** are to **cactus** as **roots** are to **plant.**
- ❒ **Spines** are to **cactus** as **leaves** are to **plant.**

STEAM Project-Based Learning GRADES 1–6

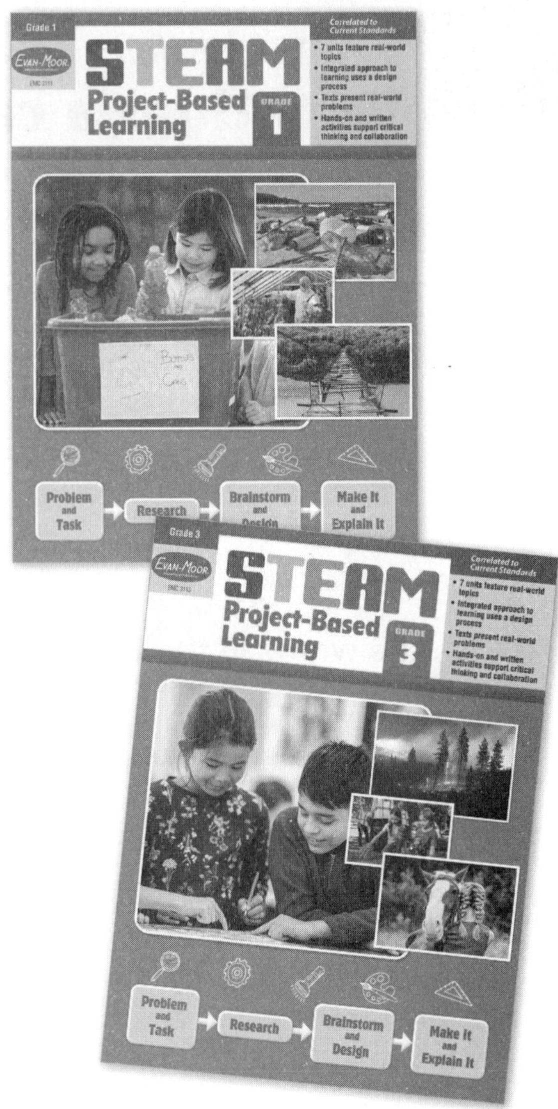

Real-World Learning for Tomorrow's Leaders!

STEAM is an approach to project-based learning that uses **Science, Technology, Engineering, the Arts, and Mathematics** to engage children in empathizing, thinking critically, collaborating, and coming up with solutions to solve real-world problems.

Each robust unit in this classroom resource focuses on a hands-on STEAM project that encourages students to enjoy the journey of creating and sharing his or her solutions to help create a better world.

128 reproducible pages.
Correlated to current standards.

Grade 3

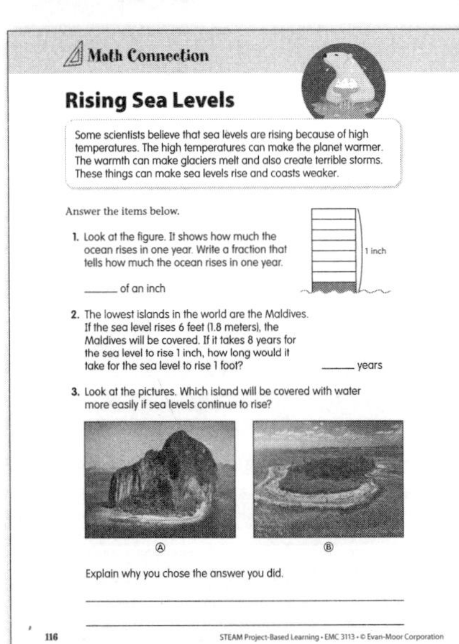

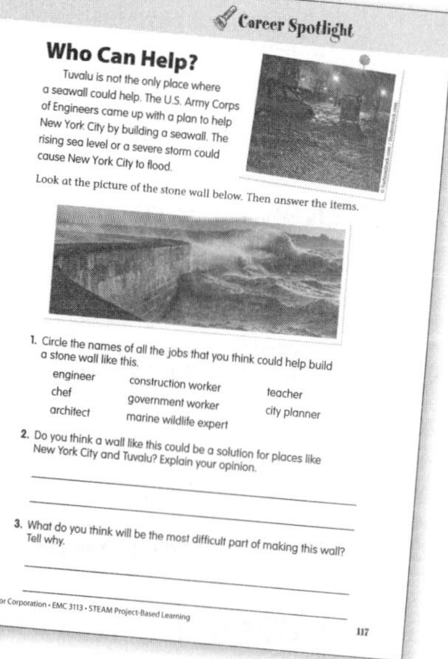

Teacher's Edition*

Grade 1	EMC 3111
Grade 2	EMC 3112
Grade 3	EMC 3113
Grade 4	EMC 3114
Grade 5	EMC 3115
Grade 6	EMC 3116

**Available in print and e-book*